D1055993

More praise from the business community for MANAGING KNOCK YOUR SOCKS OFF SERVICE:

"This entertaining resource provides the tools to reduce the art of 'delivering' Knock Your Socks Off Service into the science of 'managing' the process. I expected a great book from Bell and Zemke, but this work exceeded my expectations."

> John H. Longstreet
> General Manager
> Harvey Hotels

"If you're serious about cultivating a service climate with your employees to make a difference with your customers, this book is a must read!"

> George Vehi
> General Manager
> Rogers Cable T.V., Ltd.

"It doesn't get any better than this!! Any CEO who truly wants a service culture in his organization will make this 'text book' available to *all* of his managers. Don't worry, just give it to them and with this book they'll do the rest."

> William W. Young, Jr.
> President
> Central Maine Healthcare

"MANAGING KNOCK YOUR SOCKS OFF SERVICE provides the key link between *knowing* the importance of exemplary customer service and actually *delivering* it. Using a mixture of humor, anecdotes and practical insights, Chip Bell and Ron Zemke have provided us with an extremely useful management tool. Now, there are no more excuses for not providing superior service to all your customers."

> George E. Fuehrer
> Senior Vice President
> EnviroSource, Inc.

"Complete state-of-the-art service strategies in one small, easy-to-read book."

> Judith S. Corson
> Partner
> Custom Research Inc.

"Achieving customer satisfaction consistently is never easy. This book provides a road map, which if followed leads not only to customer satisfaction, but more important, to meeting and exceeding your customer requirements."

> David H. Radack, V.P.
> U.S. Customer Service
> Amdahl Corporation

Managing
Knock
Your
Socks
Off
Service

Chip R. Bell
and
Ron Zemke

amacom
American Management Association

New York • Atlanta • Boston • Chicago • Kansas City
San Francisco • Washington, D.C.
Brussels • Toronto • Mexico City

This book is available at a special
discount when ordered in bulk quantities.
For information, contact Special Sales Department,
AMACOM, a division of American Management Association,
135 West 50th Street, New York, NY 10020.

This publication is designed to provide accurate and authoritative
information in regard to the subject matter covered. It is sold with
the understanding that the publisher is not engaged in rendering
legal, accounting, or other professional service. If legal advice or
other expert assistance is required, the services of a competent
professional person should be sought.

Library of Congress Cataloging-in-Publication Data

Bell, Chip R.
    Managing knock your socks off service / Chip R. Bell and
Ron Zemke.
        p. cm.
    Includes bibliographical references.
    ISBN 0–8144–7784–4
    1. Customer service.   I. Zemke, Ron.   II. Title.
HF5415.5.B436 1992
658.8'12—dc20   91–48064
                                                              CIP

Managing Knock Your Socks Off Service® is a registered trademark
of Performance Research Associates, Inc.

© 1992 Performance Research Associates, Inc.
All rights reserved.
Printed in the United States of America.
Artwork © 1992 John Bush

This publication may not be reproduced, stored in a retrieval system, or
transmitted in whole or in part, in any form or by any means, electronic,
mechanical, photocopying, recording, or otherwise, without the prior
written permission of AMACOM, a division of American Management
Association, 135 West 50th Street, New York, NY 10020.

Printing number

10 9 8 7 6

Contents

Our Thanks   vii

Introduction   ix

Imperative 1: Find and Retain Quality People   **1**

1   Select Slowly . . . and Hire Carefully   3
2   Paying Attention to Employee Retention   11
3   What Leads to Longevity?   17

Imperative 2: Know Your Customers Intimately   **23**

4   Good Service Is Whatever the Customer Says It Is   25
5   Good Enough . . . Isn't   31
6   Listening Is a Contact Sport   37
7   A Complaining Customer Is Your Best Friend   43
8   Little Things Mean a Lot   50
9   Building Service Partnerships   57

Imperative 3: Focus on "Purpose"   **63**

10   The Power of Purpose   65
11   Getting Your Focus Down on Paper   69
12   A Service Strategy Statement Sampler   74

**Imperative 4: Make Your Service Delivery System
ETDBW (Easy to Do Business With)**   **83**

13   Bad Systems Stop Good People   85
14   Fix the System, Not the People   90

15 Measure and Manage From the Customer's Point
    of View   95
16 Add Value: The Milk and Cookies Principle   102
17 Make Recovery a Point of Pride . . . and a Part of
    Your System   107
18 If It Ain't Broke . . . Fix It   113

Imperative 5: Train and Support   **123**

19 Start on Day One (When Their Hearts and Minds
    Are Malleable)   125
20 Training Creates Competence, Confidence, and
    Longevity   130
21 Making Training Stick   137
22 Thinking and Acting Like a Coach   143

Imperative 6: Involve and Empower   **153**

23 Empowerment Is Not a Gift   155
24 Removing the Barriers to Empowerment   161

**Imperative 7: Recognize, Reward, and Celebrate
Success**   **167**

25 Recognition and Reward: Fueling the Fires of
    Service Success   169
26 Feedback: Breakfast, Lunch, and Dinner of
    Champions   174
27 Interpersonal Feedback   180
28 Celebrate Success   184

**Imperative 8: Your Most Important Management
Mission: Set the Tone and Lead the Way**   **191**

29 Observation Is More Powerful Than Conversation   193
30 Reinventing Your Service System   196
31 The Journey From Boss to Leader   201

    For More Reading on Service   207

OUR THANKS

Taking a book from rough idea to polished publication is an interdependent effort. We have many to thank for their energies.

Dick Schaaf was our Minneapolis editor and vernacular engineer. His superb wordsmithing made ideas sound wonderful. We are grateful for his excellent craftmanship and "beyond the call of duty" dedication.

Kristin Anderson was our super researcher, unearthing novel illustrations important in helping you find relevance and application in what we communicate. Jill Applegate typed the manuscript over and over and over—all the while telling us how much she liked what she was typing. John Bush never ceased to amaze us with his "capture the essence" creative illustrations.

Andrea Pedolsky, our AMACOM editor, was a model of stoic calm and perserverance on the sea of craziness and ever-moving deadlines we created.

We owe a special thanks to Nancy Bell and Susan Zemke, who not only gave us patience, compassionate critique, and undying love, but frequently "took up the slack" to provide us valuable space for focus on this book.

Finally, we wish to thank the many client organizations and workshop participants who gave us the opportunity to test and refine the ideas and techniques in this book.

Chip R. Bell	Ron Zemke
Charlotte, NC	Minneapolis, MN

Introduction

Four words capture what today's customer wants from your organization: *faster—better—their way*. There is no mistaking the message. The company that can shave delivery and turnaround time, provide better quality, and tailor its products and services to the customer's precise needs is a company to be reckoned with. Add one more dimension, and you have a company with an insurmountable edge on the competition. That dimension?

▲ Knock Your Socks Off Customer Service

The Economics of KYSOS

Providing outstanding customer service as part of the "package" you present to your customers pays and pays well. Studies done by business economists show that companies rated high on the quality of their customer service:

- Keep customers longer—50 percent longer or more.
- Have lower sales and marketing costs—20 percent to 40 percent lower.
- Experience higher return on sales—7 percent to 12 percent higher.
- Have better net profits—7 percent to 17 percent better.

There is another economic dimension to good service. When customers are pleased with the way they are treated, employees are frequently more satisfied with their jobs and content to stay with the organization. Why? Simple! Who wants to spend their working hours in an organization customers hate? And who isn't motivated by a customer's thanks—and a manager's "job well done"?

The Geography of KYSOS

In principle, Knock Your Socks Off Service is pretty simple: Make sure you know what your customer wants and expects of you; be flexible in meeting those demands; treat the customer like a partner rather than an adversary or end-user; and work like heck to make it easy for the customer to do business with you.

It's a mission that's easy to talk. But hard to walk.

Why is providing great service so difficult—more difficult, some would say, than making a great product? Think about the simple haircut, a service so common and ordinary we just take it for granted. It is a good illustration of just how different and difficult creating world-class, customer-pleasing service can be.

If you are a barber/beautician/stylist, you are very much at the behest of whoever walks in the door. No rejecting the raw material or sending it back to the vendor. No way to say, "I'm sorry, sir/ma'am, but your head is out of round and your hair is just too thin. We don't work with substandard material." Nor do you have more than partial control over standards. The *customer* controls the standards. And the one who walks in the door with a copy of *Esquire* or *Vogue* or *Self* or *Fortune* with a favorite photo of Madonna or Whitney Houston or Bruce Willis or Eddie Murphy circled has clear expectations in mind, realistic or not—and will hold you to them.

On top of that, customers don't leave their heads for you to work on and come back at 5 P.M. to survey your work. Oh, no, they hop up in the chair, look into the back bar mirror, and "help" you do your job: "Careful! Not too short" . . . "Now don't make the part too wide" . . . "Not too close on the sideburns, full on the sides though." They stay right there in your factory and tell you how to take care of business for them.

And when you've finished, they are only conditionally

satisfied with the job you've done. The final, *final* evaluation must wait until they see how their spouse, family, friends, co-workers, and casual passersby react to the "new do"—and until they've had a crack at reproducing your styling excellence in their own bathroom mirror after a hot steamy shower.

That, in a nutshell, is the reality of delivering quality service today. It must be done one customer and one encounter at a time, each and every time, to the specifications of that one customer—if you are going to have a chance of getting that customer back again.

As a manager, you know how important it is that the people who deal with your customers each and every day are successful at each and every opportunity, and how difficult it can be to ensure that that happens. You are, after all, working with people, not machinery, and quality is more complicated than having the right combination of raw material, machinery, and control procedures.

For eight years, we've studied successful service companies in the United States, Canada, Europe, Australia, and South America, looking for their secrets, the things (often little, subtle things) they do that distinguish them from their poorer performing competitors. In 1989 we added a survey database to help us learn even more. Today we have detailed surveys from 37,000 managers, supervisors, and frontline service providers in over 200 organizations. Our interviews, case histories, and surveys convinced us that managers at every level in every walk of these organizations create superior service by:

1. Finding and retaining quality people
2. Knowing their customers intimately
3. Focusing their units on organizational purpose
4. Creating easy-to-do-business-with delivery systems
5. Training and supporting employees
6. Involving and empowering employees
7. Recognizing and rewarding good performance and celebrating success
8. Setting the tone and leading the way through personal example.

A word about our starting point—people. If we've learned one thing from the thousands of managers we've worked with in ferreting out the keys to successful service delivery, it is this: Start with good people or else don't start. It takes bright, savvy, well-trained frontliners to make your service strategy a reality. Yes, the other seven factors (which we refer to as operational imperatives) are important. But those factors assume that you have hired people capable of, and willing to, do the job, people who are eager to learn and excited about the idea of helping you create a special organization . . . an organization distinguished by Knock Your Socks Off Service.

Imperative 1
Find and Retain
Quality People

Hire good people and work like heck to keep them on the payroll. Knock Your Socks Off Service starts here or it doesn't start at all.

If you are really serious about serving customers better than your competition, you have to start with people who are willing and able to make that happen. Hiring well means being highly selective. When it comes to creating and maintaining a positive relationship with customers, hiring *nobody* is sometimes better than settling for the first warm body that volunteers to show up for eight hours. You can't end up with satisfied, loyal customers if you don't start with quality people—the kind of people who get as big a kick out of delivering great service as customers do receiving it. Period.

But this is a two-act play. Once found and brought on board, quality people must be kept on board. That means orienting them carefully—so they come to understand just exactly what you mean by high-quality service. It also means training them fully in the knowledge and skills necessary for success, giving them challenging assignments, and keeping them interested in the work of the organization. And sometimes it means paying them better than the competition is willing to.

It also means growing them, rewarding and recognizing their accomplishments—sometimes individually, sometimes as a group. It means celebrating their efforts when they go "one step beyond" for their customers.

If you seriously intend to distinguish yourself from the competition through smooth, seamless Knock Your Socks Off Service, you won't accomplish that hiring from the labor pool from hell or by maintaining a payroll that turns over faster than dishwashers in a Las Vegas hotel.

> You start with good people, you train and motivate them, you give them an opportunity to advance, then the organization succeeds.
>
> —J. W. "Bill" Marriott, Jr.
> Chairman and CEO, Marriott Corporation

1

Select Slowly ... and Hire Carefully

We don't start out with the assumption that our company
is for everybody.

—William G. McGowan
Chairman, MCI Communications Corp.

On Interstate 4 southwest of Orlando, Florida, a striking gold and purple building fronts the freeway. A big—very big—sign defines it in one eloquently simple word: CASTING. It's the Walt Disney World personnel office. That one word says a lot about not just Disney but all companies that are focused on becoming known for Knock Your Socks Off Service. They don't "hire" people for "jobs." They "cast" performers in a "role."

In service-focused companies, customer service jobs are thought of less like factory work and much more like theater. At a play, the audience files in, the curtain goes up, the actors make their entrances and speak their lines—and if each and every cast member, not to mention the writer, director, stage-hands, costumers, makeup artists, and lighting technicians, have prepared themselves and the theater well, the audience enjoys the show and tells others about it. Then again, despite the proven talents of individual members of the cast or the presence of an award-winning director or the skills of the backstage crew, the whole thing can be a magnificent flop if just one person fails to do a job on which everyone else depends.

3

In today's service-driven business world, you are more director than boss, more choreographer than administrator. Your frontline people are the actors, and your customers are the audience for whom they must perform. Everyone else is support crew, charged with making sure the theater is right, the sets ready, the actors primed and prepared. You have to prepare your cast to know their cues, hit their marks, deliver their lines, and improvise when another cast member or someone in the audience disrupts the carefully plotted flow of the performance. And, of course, once the curtain goes up, all you can do is watch and whisper from the wings. You're not allowed on stage. You'd just get in the way!

Taking Your Time

If you're casting for a performance, obviously success or failure is going to hinge on whom you put in which roles. Given all the currents flowing under and around the hiring process today, the last thing you want to do is rush into a decision you're literally going to have to live with for years. Once the casting decision has been made, your entire production's reviews are going to depend on the person you've chosen for the role. It's as easy to be taken in by a handsome external facade as by a well-proportioned résumé. Neither may be truly indicative of whether someone can play the part the way you need it to be played.

Yes, the show must go on. But if you've been building a good, versatile cast, you should have understudies ready to fill in while you look for new additions to your service repertory crew. Don't rush the process. Invest the time and effort needed to get the right person. When you do, you'll find you're in good company.

A few years ago, we researched the business practices of some 400 exemplary service performers—the kinds of businesses that expose the oft-heard excuse "You just can't get good help these days" for the cheap alibi it really is. In company after company, we found painstaking thoroughness built in to every step of the selection process:

- For the grand opening of the Grand Hyatt Wailea, one of the crown jewel Hawaiian resorts, 6,000 people were screened to fill 1,200 jobs.
- When Nordstrom opened its first East Coast store in Tyson's Corner, Virginia, it interviewed 3,000 people to fill 400 frontline jobs.
- Applicants for positions with St. Petersburg-based Florida Power Corporation attend job preview days where experienced performers demonstrate everything from rolling cable to answering the phone. The realistic view of the company's work helps people select the positions they're best able to fill and deselect themselves from areas where they clearly wouldn't fit.

Hiring as Casting

Filling out your service cast with people who can star in their roles is the key to success. But casting your customer service play is far more involved and difficult than hiring "somebody— anybody" to sit in a chair and answer a phone, or stand at a counter and take orders. Consider the following three key differences between merely filling a slot and getting someone capable of playing a part.

1. *Great service performers must be able to create a relationship with the audience.* From the customer's standpoint, every performance is "live" and hence unique. It earns the best reviews when it appears genuine, perhaps even spontaneous. And it should never be rigidly scripted—certainly not canned.

▲ *Implication:* Customer service cast members must have good person-to-person skills; their speaking, listening, chatting, and interacting styles should seem natural and friendly and appropriate to the situation— neither stiff and formal nor overly familiar.

2. *Great service performers must be able to handle pressure.* There are many kinds of pressure—pressure of the clock,

pressure from customers, pressure from other players in the service cast, and pressure from the desire to do a good job for both customer and company even though the two may be in conflict.

▲ *Implication*: Members of the customer service cast must be good at handling their own emotions, calm under fire, and not susceptible to "catching the stress virus" from upset customers. At the same time, they have to acknowledge and support their customers' upsets and problems and demonstrate a desire to help resolve the situation in the best way possible.

3. *Great service performers must be able to learn new scripts.* They have to be flexible enough to adjust to changes in the cast and conditions surrounding them, make changes in their own performance as conditions warrant, and still seem natural and knowledgeable.

▲ *Implication*: Customer service cast members need to be lifelong learners—curious enough to learn from the environment as well as the classroom, comfortable enough to be constantly looking for new ways to enhance their performance, confident enough to indulge the natural curiosity to ask, "Why is that?" and poke around the organization to learn how things really work. Those who are comfortable with change and handle it well can be the most helpful to customers and need minimal hand holding from their managers.

To get the right kind of people for your own service repertory company, you have to know (1) what you're looking for and (2) how to look for it.

Eight Tips for Casting Well

1. *Treat every vacancy like an open role in a play.* Define the service role you are auditioning people for in terms of the part

the new cast members must play and how they'll have to relate to the other members in the cast. Make people skills and technical knowledge of equal importance in your hiring.

2. *Identify the skills needed for the role.* Once the interview begins, it's too late to start thinking about what you want to learn. Based on the job description and your knowledge of the role you are casting, what traits or personal attributes do you want new cast members to possess? Friendliness? Courtesy? Optimism? Creativity? How will you judge the presence or absence of those traits to your satisfaction? Focus the various stages of the selection process on the real-world skills demanded by the part you're trying to fill.

3. *"Screen test" your applicants.* Consider the way applicants treat your secretary or the receptionist. That may be a good indication of how they will treat your customers and their co-workers if hired. Try role-playing difficult customer situations with applicants or posing "what would you do if" questions based on the kinds of situations likely to occur on the job. You don't want to listen just for "right" or "wrong" answers. You can train them to use the right words later. Listen for orientation and attitude.

4. *Use multiple selection methods.* Remember test anxiety in school? Job applicants get it too. Instead of sifting all applicants through one coarse screen, use a succession of fine ones to help you differentiate. Consider:

- *Multiple Interviews.* See your applicants more than once, each time with specific objectives in mind for the interview. If others in your organization are skilled interviewers, tell them what you're looking for and have them make an assessment too.
- *Peer Interviews.* In firms where teamwork is valued, it's not uncommon for cast members who will be working with whoever is hired to be trained to do short interviews of their own. Their viewpoints are highly functional. When the project has to be finished under the gun, the person *you're* hiring is someone *they'll* need to work with and depend on.

Selection Questions

There are no magic questions that automatically illustrate an applicant's character and service outlook. But there are questions that work better than others at eliciting the kind of information you need in order to make an informed hiring decision. Here are a few to use or adapt:

- What does giving the customer "superior service" mean to you?
- Tell me about a time when you went above and beyond the call of duty in serving a customer.
- When you came here today, what did you notice about our own customer service—things we did well or things we could improve on?
- We all get weary from time to time from the pressure of dealing with people. How do you stay "up," fresh and enthusiastic?
- I know I sometimes get uptight when I have to deal with an irate customer. You've had experience with difficult customers—how do you handle them?
- What do you like most about being in customer service?

- *Job-Validated Testing*. Tests that reflect the true nature of the job and assess the key skills needed to do it proficiently are valid, provided they're administered equally and fairly to everyone under consideration. Use them.
- *Job Previewing*. Let applicants spend some time seeing what they're getting themselves into. If they're serious, they'll find ways to better present their qualifications to you. If the job turns out to be something other than what they were expecting, they'll often save you the cost of a bad hire by deselecting themselves.
- *Internships*. Work/study, apprenticeship, and part-time

programs give you an opportunity to audition and evaluate candidates over a predetermined period of time while getting some work done, too. If you like what you see—and they like what they do—you're already through the break-in period. If not, you both have a graceful way out.

5. *Emphasize mutual selection*. Applicants need to make as good a selection decision as you do. Just as you want to pick the right person, you gain by helping them pick the right position and organization. If they make a poorly informed decision and discover it only after being on board for a while, you will end up with a competent but unhappy camper.

6. *Consider nontraditional sources*. The traditional entry-level work force is shrinking. But the proportion of Americans over the age of fifty is growing. On the factory floor, where physical strength and stamina were important, workers with physical disabilities were a potential liability. In the computer-driven service workplace, few impairments are truly disabling. Remember that training can build skills: When you find people with the fire and drive and work ethic to succeed, don't see them as dull rocks because they are disabled or "different," but as diamonds in the rough. With the right cut and polish, their real potential is revealed.

7. *Recruit actively*. Good people may not always find you. Sometimes, you have to find them. Where have your best people been coming from? Are there others back there equally ready and willing to do the job for you? When you encounter someone who serves you well, don't be shy about handing them your business card and suggesting they get in touch the next time they're ready to make a change. Reward your people—pay 'em a bounty—for bringing in friends, former colleagues, even relatives who are capable of filling roles in your production.

8. *Hire people like the job, not like you*. Internally focused corporations have cultures. Externally focused organizations have whatever kind of people it takes to dazzle the customer and bring them back again. It's very human to overlay personal

beliefs, values, likes, and dislikes on the selection process, but it's seldom in the best interest of the customer to do so. Remember the words of economist Leo Rosten: "First-rate men hire first-rate men. Second-rate men hire third-rate men." (We're sure he'd have said "people" if he said this today.)

Success on the "Customer Service Stage" takes a great cast, a super script, great support, and great direction. Never compromise on casting. It's critical to everything else in the production.

> All the world's a stage, and all the men and women merely players: . . .
>
> —William Shakespeare, *As You Like It*

2

Paying Attention to Employee Retention

I can think of no company that has found a way to look after external customers while abusing internal customers. The process of meeting customer needs begins internally.

—Tom Peters
Management guru

It used to be so much easier. You needed a body—any body would do. So you called Personnel. Someone ran an ad. People sent résumés and filled out application forms. Someone screened the candidates and selected those who seemed most likely to fit into the corporate culture. You interviewed two, maybe three, people—mostly to double-check what was on the applications and make sure none of them had two heads or tended to scratch in embarrassing places. Then you hired one. A week or two later, she showed up, signed a batch of forms, picked up her employee manual, and went to sit next to Sally or John or Mary to learn the ropes for a couple of days. And that was that. End of story. If she didn't work out, you simply made her available to other employers (or transferred her someplace where her influence would be less noxious) and tried again.

No more. People can no longer be treated as interchangeable parts, essential but essentially similar cogs for the assembly line. Now people are *both* the assembly line and the product. How well they perform is a key component in your ability to satisfy customers enough for them to want to do business with you again. As we've all been learning (often to our dismay) in recent years, the odds against finding the right amount of the right kinds of people are much higher today than ever before.

- The U.S. Government projects that some 16 million new jobs will be created by the turn of the century, yet only 14 million new workers will be wading into the labor pool in the same time frame.
- The average U.S. high school graduate can't do a three-step math problem, yet computers, statistical process control, qualitative measurement, and technical expertise are basic components of the workplace.
- About 20 percent of the people who show up looking for a job can't understand the instructions "In case of emergency, pull handle," yet they have to be able to read, respond to, educate, and meet the rising expectations of ever more demanding customers on a minute-by-minute and day-by-day basis.

Despite the economic bumps experienced in the opening years of the 1990s, we're in a tight labor market—and one that will get not only tighter but progressively older, more diverse, and less interested in traditional low-pay, low-status, low-prestige, entry-level jobs. Your challenge? Find people who can do the job today . . . *and* can keep learning so they can do the job tomorrow . . . *and* can handle customers like a million-dollar salesperson . . . *and* can solve customer problems . . . *and* will act on their own in unique and unusual situations . . . *and* remain poised under pressure . . . *and* can be relied upon to act in the best interest of the customer without compromising the company.

Of course, once you find these paragons of service virtue, they must be willing to take the job . . . *and* be able to work the hours it demands, including evenings, weekends, and the

other odd times your customers think they want to be served
. . . *and* be prepared to accept a compensation package you can
afford . . . *and* be imbued with a commitment to stay with the
task at hand that will allow them to gain the experience to do
it better . . . *and* be balanced enough to do the work without
burning out on the steady diet of stress and tension that so
often goes with frontline service.

Oh yes, you also have to be able to find, hire, and retain
people with these unique and special skills without inadver-
tently violating one or more of the dozen and a half laws and
guidelines that protect job hunters and employees alike from
unfair treatment—and without giving them reason to start
looking for greener pastures before the pressure-sensitive ink
starts to set on their first payroll form.

Keeping People Builds Profits

Distinctive service begins with hiring people who are a cut or
three above average. That's the easy part. Once you've got 'em,
you have to work like hell to keep them. Not just because
they're good people, but because they're your real profit gen-
erators. Writing in the *Harvard Business Review*, Leonard A.
Schlesinger and James L. Heskett put the issue in bottom-line
terms:

- At Marriott, they report, a 10 percent decrease in employee turnover has been found to correlate with a 1–3-
  percent decrease in lost customers and a $50 million–
  $100 million increase in revenues.
- The connection between losing people, losing customers, and losing revenue is a crucial one. In another study
  on the economic impact of customer retention, they
  found that every 5 percent increase in customer retention
  generates a corresponding "bump" in profitability that
  ranges from 25 percent to 125 percent.

Other pacesetting service companies have learned similar
lessons, and many are documenting similar returns on their

human resources investment. They're using training not only to educate but to motivate. They're using dual career tracks to keep top performers doing what they do best while providing them with satisfying growth and financial rewards. They're educating managers to the new realities of the work force to make sure they understand that service people bruise easily and that good ones are too precious to waste through managerial abuse.

As the labor market, especially the market for top-notch service people, continues to tighten, more and more managers are making the connection between satisfied customers who keep coming back and the loyal, motivated people who provide the service that brings those customers back. Increasingly, keeping good people is treated as a critical concern by the service elite, recession or boom.

- At Walt Disney World, job rotation, cross-training, and the clearly observable fact that the road to management starts at the front line combine to give the controlled entertainment king a frontline turnover rate less than half the theme park industry average.
- At Precision LensCrafters, the "glasses in about an hour" people, career movement opportunities, sales incentives, and a strong "in-group" corporate culture keep turnover low despite a very competitive, high-pressure retail setting.
- In Embassy Suites properties, frontline people are rewarded with raises for learning new jobs through cross-training that's available to them even when no immediate openings are projected. This learning-and-earning incentive keeps turnover of frontliners among the lowest in the industry (and provides an emergency staffing pool ready to respond at a moment's notice).

Dollars Plus Sense

The data assembled by Schlesinger and Heskett in their *Harvard Business Review* article make it clear that playing the "find-and-keep quality people" game not only improves overall service satisfaction results but is actually *less costly* than continuing to churn cheap help. The long-running saga of St. Petersburg-based Florida Power Corporation certainly corroborates their contention.

According to Walt Thurn, manager of employee development, Florida Power's commitment to employee retention dates back to 1983, when the company concluded that it couldn't hope to improve service quality with a 48 percent annual turnover rate among field service reps. In 1984 the company installed a new, tougher selection system. Predictably, the number of applicants rejected skyrocketed, but that wasn't the only number that changed. In short order, the influence of hiring better people and working to retain them shrunk the turnover rate to 9 percent annually. That, says Thurn, translates to annual savings of more than $2 million in employment costs: the cost of constantly hiring, training, losing, and replacing people.

Meanwhile, the "new look" field reps are receiving more training and advancing faster than any group of service technicians in the past twenty-five years. Best of all, customer satisfaction ratings are the highest and customer complaint rates are the lowest of any utility in the Southeast.

Selling Employees on Service

Despite the evidence to the contrary, we constantly hear managers grouse that service work is work nobody really wants to do. On closer examination, we think you'll find that service is work we—as managers—have *turned into* work nobody wants to do. We saw this illustrated in Australia not long ago, when Daimaru, a Japanese retailer, opened its first "offshore" store in Melbourne, right across the street from Coles Myer, Ltd., the largest retailer in Australia.

To set the stage, understand first of all that in Australian merchandising, sales clerks, called "shop assistants," are the lowest of the low. Low pay. Low status. Low self-esteem. Low perch on the totem pole. Daimaru clearly thought through the implications of that on employee selection and retention before placing its first help wanted ad in the local papers. With typical Japanese modesty, the ad announced that Daimaru had the great good fortune to be opening a new store in Melbourne but that it wouldn't be hiring any "shop assistants" to work in it. Rather, the company noted, it was looking for "1,000 people who would like a career in retailing."

Stuff and nonsense, right? If that's so, then what accounts for the fact that about 3 A.M. on the day when interviews were to commence, a line started forming. By the end of the first day, more than 10,000 applications had been filled out. For one store. For jobs "nobody wants to do."

> In 1986 employee turnover was 220 percent. We knew we had to change. We would hire only the best, pay them to be the best, motivate the heck out of them, and make them so happy that their energy and enthusiasm just couldn't help but result in great service. In the first three months of this year, turnover was 39 percent in an industry that averages 250 percent.
>
> —Keith Dunn
> Founder and CEO, McGuffey's Restaurant

3

What Leads to Longevity?

The deepest principle of human nature is a craving to be appreciated.

—William James
Father of American Psychology

Why does turnover matter? It matters because companies that retain their proven service performers retain their customers as well. The connection is direct and powerful and cuts across virtually every dividing line: industry, size of company, scale of market, you name it. It's not difficult to see why.

- Customers want and value reliability and consistency in their service experiences with you. From the *customer* standpoint, dealing with experienced people is basic to building a relationship—a true partnership. If customers can deal with the same people who took care of them last time, they can expect the same things that went right then to go right again. When each new encounter is handled by a strange face or voice, your organization has to demonstrate its reliability and consistency all over again.
- Teamwork comes from working together long enough to learn the strengths and weaknesses, special quirks, and predictable habits of other members of the team. As service becomes more complex and service relationships

17

grow to touch multiple levels and layers in the organization, internal coordination becomes an important factor in external satisfaction.

- Finally, experience is still the best teacher—no classroom session or three-ring binder full of job aids and policy statements can hope to replicate the database that resides squarely between your employees' ears. Your true "personnel cost" is much more than a salary total. It's every dime, every minute, every ounce of energy anyone in your organization has spent recruiting, interviewing, hiring, training, supervising, helping out, working with, and profiting from your people.

Customers Are Watching

Just as your style of service determines whether you'll retain a customer, your style of managing is basic to the retention and service achievements of your people. Yet we all know that there are managers who still use their authority as a club to beat the drive, the initiative, the sense of fun, and the risk-taking out of people.

Not only does this have a profound effect on the people we manage, it also has an effect—typically more direct than we give it credit for—on customers. If you've ever stood at a checkout counter, held captive by a supervisor who deems it more important that the clerk explain vague chicken scratches on yesterday's timecard than take your money, you've seen the downside of service management in action.

In several studies, researchers Benjamin Schneider and Richard Bowen have shown that *customer service satisfaction* is directly related to *employee job satisfaction*. Their work, done both jointly and independently over a ten-year period, points to a number of specific ways that job satisfaction is tied to customer satisfaction:

1. Customers "see into" the organization through a unique window: the actions and words of frontline employees. They assume the attitude and treatment they experience at the

front line of an organization is an accurate representation of the way the organization wants customers to be treated.

2. The treatment customers experience, however, reflects the treatment employees receive from their managers. The "kick-the-cat" phenomenon is real. If you're at the front line and your boss gives you a hard time, you pass that treatment on—sometimes to other employees, sometimes to family, and sometimes to customers.

3. On the whole, employees desire to give good service and receive customer accolades for it. When conditions prevent or prohibit them from doing what they believe to be in the best interests of the customer, they become defensive and prickly.

On the positive side, Schnieder and Bowen have found that employees and customers both rate service quality highest in branches where (1) there is an enthusiastic service emphasis, (2) branch managers emphasize the importance of service to branch success, (3) there is an active effort to retain all accounts, not just "high net" customers, (4) the number of well-trained frontline people at the branch is sufficient to provide customers good service, (5) equipment is well maintained and supplies are plentiful, and (6) employees believe they have a reasonable opportunity for career advancement in the organization.

Only when the economics of the workplace are such that there are few jobs and a lot of people wanting them will people put up with anything just to eat. But as soon as conditions improve, the ones with gumption and initiative—the ones you really want to keep because they're the hardest to find and replace—will be gone. The question you have to answer is whether you want to depend on crisis conditions for employee retention or look for a better way.

How to Retain

As a manager, you have a variety of weapons to use to keep your own employees coming back:

• *Compensation.* Money, the Pollyannas among us note, isn't everything . . . to which the cynics promptly reply, "Okay, but it's a very close second to whatever's first." Service-distinctive organizations not uncommonly pay above the average for their industry, using the tactic (1) to attract good people and (2) to keep them from seeking greener pastures. Federal Express package sorters start out at about double the minimum wage, and even part-timers are eligible for bonuses and profit-sharing. Top sales associates in Nordstrom department stores can earn well in excess of $50,000 a year.

• *Special Treatment.* In lieu of money, respect for individual concerns can compensate in a variety of ways. Instead of forcing everyone to fit into the same employee box, recognize that people each need and value different things. For parents with young children, for example, it may be flexibility around day care; for parents whose children are a little older, it may be the opportunity to attend an occasional school program in the middle of the afternoon.

• *Special Contracts and Perks.* Tie specific types of performance achievements to specific payoffs, whether monetary or symbolic. A "piece of the action"—the increased revenue from a formerly static account that's now growing, or the savings from a suggestion—tells your people you value their efforts. Similarly, a special parking space, tickets to athletic or cultural events, enhanced discounts on the company's products and services, and other "spiffs" keep them from feeling taken for granted.

• *Training.* For today's knowledge workers, one of the most enlivening and enriching experiences is training that helps them do their jobs better. They know performance counts, that in many cases they're being judged on how well their customers say they're serving. Developing new talents or getting a refresher on old ones helps them stay on top of their game. It also communicates the organization's continuing commitment to them.

• *Cross-Training.* The more hats your people can wear, the more valuable they can be to the organization. If their current specialty goes away or is de-emphasized, they know and you know that they're ready and able to fill an emerging need instead of filling out an applica.ion for unemployment insurance. What's more, having people pretrained for other jobs helps you meet unexpected demands, from the need to replace someone who departs unexpectedly, to coping with the occasional (and unpredictable) overload situation, to the ability to respond quickly to new demands and opportunities.

• *Lateral Job Movement.* The most exciting and fulfilling job becomes stagnant and predictable over time. At Southern California Gas, lateral "developmental assignments" are used to challenge, reward, and motivate people who can't move up (because so many layers of "up" have been eliminated in recent years). Giving your people the opportunity to move laterally not only gives them a chance to rise to a new challenge but helps them gain a new perspective on what they've been doing.

• *Empowerment.* According to Richard Leider, author of *Intrapreneuring*, the biggest problem today isn't burnout—it's rustout. So many people in our organizations are capable of doing so much more than we've ever asked (or allowed) them to do. So let 'em. The more ownership they assume for the responsibilities built into their job, the more likely they are to stay with it, no matter (and perhaps because of) how challenging they find it.

• *Reward and Recognition.* What gets rewarded gets repeated. If you want people to stay and grow with you, recognize and reward them, not just for their years of service but for their accomplishments along the way. For most people, the research shows that being thanked for a job well done is a more powerful motivator than money. It says you're paying attention to their individual (or team) performance, that you recognize how hard they're working, how much they're contributing, how valuable they are.

• *Celebration.* If people don't, won't, or can't laugh in the workplace, there's something seriously wrong in the workplace. When it goes well, make a point of celebrating the victory—and the people who made it possible. Recognize and thank everyone involved for their effort. That'll send them back into the game determined to win again and proud to be playing on a winning team.

We have a belief that our guests will only receive the kind
of treatment we want them to receive if the cast members
receive that same kind of treatment from their managers.

Walt Disney World Handbook

Imperative 2
Know Your Customers Intimately

You subscribe to all the trade journals. You do an annual survey of your customers. The company even has done some market research, a couple of surveys, some focus groups. You sit next to the people on the phones from time to time. You yourself jump in and work with tough customer problems when asked. You regularly talk with the salespeople to learn what they are hearing from their customers, prospects, and suspects.

You *are* close to the customer—right? Perhaps. And then again, perhaps not.

Knowing your customer intimately means more than having a passing acquaintance with the market research of your industry or company. It means spending time listening to, understanding, and responding—often in unique and creative ways—to your customers'

evolving needs and shifting expectations. Knowing your customer intimately means that people at *all* levels of the organization find time to meet with, listen to, and learn from customers in highly focused ways. Knowing your customer intimately means knowing each other's business so well that you can anticipate each other's problems and opportunities—and can work on solutions and strategies together.

> Listening to customers must become everyone's business. With competitors moving ever faster, the race will go to those who listen (and respond) most intently.

> —Tom Peters
> *Thriving on Chaos*

4

Good Service Is Whatever the Customer Says It Is

The customer expects you to perform. And the word "perform" doesn't mean "perfect form." It means "purr for 'em!"

—Bill Daniel
William Daniel Construction, Charlotte, North Carolina

Every couple of years, Burger King dusts off and replays one of its more memorable commercial taglines: HAVE IT YOUR WAY. It's a good line—at once the most beguiling promise and the greatest challenge of the U.S. service economy in the last decade of the twentieth century.

What it really says is that sometimes $N = 1$. In some instances, you tailor a service delivery system—from operating focus to the standards that define success—to meet the unique needs and expectations of just *one* customer. And the only way to do that is to know, in precise detail, exactly how each customer defines superior service. According to popular author Harvey Mackay's formula, there are sixty-seven different things worth knowing about your customers on an individual basis, from whether they'd rather have you call them early in the morning or late in the afternoon to their birthdays, hobbies, and interests.

Today, segmentation and niche marketing are the name of the game in virtually every industry sector. Customers are no longer shapeless, featureless mass markets. They're specific, small groups with their own unique view of what constitutes quality service. What they want and how they want it and how they do or don't get it add up to an index of service satisfaction that ultimately determines whether they'll ever come back and do business with you again. And if they don't want to come back, you're going to have serious problems being a business, whatever business you're in.

Love That Customer

Stew Leonard, chairman and patron saint of Stew Leonard's Dairy Store in Norwalk, Connecticut, is about as energetic and inspiring a leader as you can find. He rushes around his store gladhanding customers, soliciting their feedback, ringing up sales, helping lost-looking customers find what they're in search of, thumping employees on the back, and generally energizing everyone in the place. When he speaks to groups, as he often does, one of his favorite phrases is, "Ya gotta love that customer!"

Why? Consider the perspective of Robert A. "Bob" Peterson, who holds the John T. Stuart III Centennial Chair in Business Administration at the University of Texas, Austin. His opinion, based on his own research, is that "love that customer" is pretty powerful stuff.

For years, Peterson was troubled that so many people were talking about the joys of customer satisfaction, but his research wasn't showing a very strong connection between satisfaction and retention—repeat business. He found that in most surveys of customer satisfaction, something around 85 percent of an organization's customers claimed to be satisfied with the service they received but still showed a willingness to wander away to other providers if the mood or the price or the color of the advertising banner were right.

Peterson believes that we have undervalued the emotional aspects of customer service; that there is a highly personal, subjective agenda that we both fail to ask about in customer research and fail to deal with in service delivery. Only by adding words like *love* and *hate* to our surveys, and having the audacity to stand up to the need to incorporate much stronger feelings than *like* and *satisfaction* in our objectives, can we get a handle on this crucial component of customer loyalty. And the only way to get to the heart of the matter is by getting our information straight from customers: from their own selfish (and sometimes flawed) perspectives, based on their own experiences, expressed in their own words.

The payoff is the kind of in-depth understanding that can help nurture a truly productive relationship—or save one from going bad. Peterson believes that customers with strong feelings about the organization are the most predictable customers. "Customers who feel strongly about your organization—positively or negatively—are the customers *most likely* and *least likely* to do business with you again," he says.

And that's where we make the Stew Leonard connection. It's an adjunct of the Rule of Psychological Reciprocity: If you don't show interest in your customers, they won't show interest in you. If you don't trust them, they won't trust you. And if you don't care passionately, sincerely, constantly about not just meeting but exceeding their needs, they won't see you as being any better or any worse than any other organization they have done business with. They most certainly won't fall in love with your organization.

In short, "Ya gotta love that customer" if you expect them to love you back.

Romancing the Customer

Even in traditional manufacturing (and manufacturing-style services), where "careful is correct and rational is right" has long been the managerial axiom, service quality is being recognized as the marketing edge that can differentiate one commodity offering from another. The service tide in which we've all been swept up makes it imperative that we pay increasing attention to whatever it takes, one-on-one and one-by-one, to earn the love and loyalty of our customers.

We don't have the luxury of putting off this transformation. Inspired by their years of experience, well-publicized product quality improvement efforts and heightened service delivery rhetoric alike, customers are getting increasingly emotional, even passionate, about their service experiences. Listen to the raves of the Nordstrom, Lexus, L.L. Bean faithful and you'll hear more "love stories" than you'll find on the drugstore paperback rack. Listen, as well, to the tales of anger and woe told by disgruntled customers, and you'll find that novelist Stephen King doesn't have a corner on horror stories.

In this time of passion, how do you use the concept of "customer intimacy" to create long-term loyalty? Start by seeing customer transactions not as a random collection of single experiences, but as a relationship. Relationships in business, just as those in our personal lives, are built on knowledge, caring, and experience.

Know Your Customers

In *Product Development Performance*, authors Kim Clark and Takahiro Fujimoto relate how Mazda went about creating a new high-performance car for Japanese yuppies. Its first step was to put together a team of people who would design it, manufacture it, deliver it, and sell it; every step of the drawing board-to-showroom process was represented. But team members didn't sit back in the office and sift through reams of market research printouts or computer-generated engineering designs. Instead, Mazda sent them out for six months to live with the people who the company hoped would be buying the car. They went skiing with their targeted owners. They went out to eat and to the nightclubs with them. In some cases, they literally moved in and lived with them.

They came back with such an intimate understanding of what their customers wanted this new car to be and do that they created a metaphor instead of a set of expectations: The perfect car, to its customers at least, would come across as "a rugby player in an evening suit"—rugged but feline, socially recognized, polite, sportsmanlike, strong and secure, orderly, likable, bright, and elegant.

Keep Track of Your Customers

You may remember an AT&T business-to-business ad of a few years ago. Its themeline was intoned by a business-to-business service representative: "Quality is not measured by us. It's not measured by you. It's measured by your customers. If they're not happy with you, you're not happy with us."

Today, customer relationships are fluid, not static. Many, in fact, are links in a chain of customer relationships: Business-to-business service providers often are part of the service their customers provide to *their* customers. You need to be aware of where your services fit in this constantly changing spectrum of action and reaction so that, as the desires of specific customers change, you can change with them.

The consequences of failing to move with customers can be seen in virtually any field:

- As demographics showed more Americans moving into older age brackets and fewer in teenage and young adult years, many businesses developed special offerings for the 50+ crowd. Those that continued to worship youth faltered.
- As Americans have become more conscious of fat, cholesterol, and sodium in their diets, perceptive restaurateurs have added greens, chicken, and fish to their traditional beef-and-potatoes menus. Those that didn't watched increasingly empty dining rooms.
- As the consequences of smoking have become clearer, cigarette use has declined to the point that less than 30 percent of American adults now smoke. In even modest-amenity hotel chains, nonsmoking rooms are now a given—a form of enhanced service quality that actually saves money (no cigarette burns in these carpets or bedspreads, no scummy build-up on the windows or

smoke stains on the ceiling) and is noticeable when it's absent.

You need to know your customers in much greater detail than ever before. Their expectations keep changing every day, much faster than any product ever could. Their loyalty is difficult to win, easily squandered. Their voice is one well worth listening to—at least if you ever want to see them again.

The more brilliant we become on how we perform our jobs, the more inward-focused we can become and the more we need our customers' creativity. It's difficult for service people on the inside to view our service delivery system with the same naive, unbiased, and fresh perspective our customers possess.

—John Berry
COO,
Virginia Blue Cross-Blue Shield,
Roanoke, Virginia

5

Good Enough . . . Isn't

Perfection is not attainable. But if we chase perfection, we
can catch excellence.

—Vince Lombardi
Football coaching legend, Green Bay Packers

You may have heard the story about quality control and World
War II parachute packers. Supposedly, the packers felt great
pride in achieving a quality level of 99.9 percent. Surely that
was good enough for government work. Of course, for purely
selfish reasons, one paratrooper out of a thousand didn't think
of 99.9 percent as a particularly impressive achievement.

So one day the quality inspection system was changed,
and it was decreed that once a week packers would make a
jump with parachutes chosen at random from among those
packed sometime during the preceding week. The error rate
promptly disappeared, which illustrates the difference between
taking zero defects to heart and just making it a philosophical
goal to emblazon on a poster on the wall.

The idea of an "acceptable error rate" (sometimes called
an "acceptable quality level") is a quaint holdover from the
"inspect it in" era of quality. In those days, we found ways to
justify our natural human failings statistically, reasoning that
no one can possibly be perfect. So if 100 percent is unattainable,
how about making 99 percent, even 95 percent, okay? Then,
when we achieve 96.642 percent, we can have a party and
celebrate exceeding objectives.

The fact is that 96.642 percent means that 3,358 out of

every 100,000 service transactions will come up ugly. Like the luckless one-in-a-thousand paratrooper. Disgruntled customers—those who have been at the wrong end of the 96.642 percent perfect calculation—may never return either. Before we grow the business one hair's width from where it is right now, we'll first have to replace them.

In the September/October 1990 issue of the *Harvard Business Review*, Frederick F. Reichheld, a vice president in the Boston office of Bain & Company, and W. Earl Sasser, Jr., a professor at the Harvard Business School, contend that service companies are just beginning to accept the rationale that energized the quality movement in America's manufacturing sector in the 1980s: "Quality doesn't improve unless you measure it." Just as manufacturing quality efforts have been energized by the idea of zero defects, so, too, they contend, service quality efforts can and must target zero defections. Unless and until they do, we'll continue to rationalize substandard performance as somehow reasonable and acceptable.

In their words, "When manufacturers made 'zero defects' their guiding light, the quality movement took off. Service companies have their own kind of scrap heap: customers who will not come back. As the goal of manufacturing is becoming zero defects, the goal of service must become zero defections." In their *Harvard Business Review* article, Sasser and Reichheld note that companies can boost profits by almost 100 percent if they retain just 5 percent more of their customers.

The smart money, then, is on never letting go of a customer. The economics of virtually any service business will bear this out. From an internal standpoint, as customers gain experience, they learn how to make service people and systems work more time-efficiently and cost-effectively for themselves. That shows up on the bottom line, where loyal customers generate more profit over time.

- In the credit card field, the customer worth $30 per year in net revenue after a single year is worth $55 annually in year five.
- The average industrial laundry customer jumps from an initial worth of $144 per year to $256 a year in the fifth year of loyal patronage.

- The auto servicing customer who brings the company $25 annual profit will be generating $88 by the fifth year.

But the zero defections®* argument is far from a majority viewpoint. Even a good many contemporary quality mavens are hesitant to accept zero errors as an approachable goal, preferring what they term "realistic manufacturing and performance objectives." Okay. Let's play with that for a minute. Fire up your desktop calculator and let's engage in some fanciful service quality mathematics.

For starters, we have to set an ambitious but realistic error—or, conversely, success—rate. How about 99 percent? As a number, it's initially impressive. But what happens when we start applying it to the real world? Each day in the United States, for example, notes author Tom Parker in *In One Day*, 67,000 Americans undergo surgery. A 99 percent surgical success rate would mean that 66,330 come out of the anesthetic with no more serious problem than trying to figure out how to work the remote control on the hospital television set.

But what of the unfortunate few who fall into the "acceptable error" category? Each day, 670 of your friends, neighbors, relatives, and loved ones would experience complications, or die, as a result of acceptable surgical shortfalls. Assuming a six-day surgery workweek, that comes to 4,020 "realistic performance shortfalls" a week—210,000 a year! Turns out 99 percent would be a great batting average, but it makes for a less than wondrous surgical success rate.

Suppose we try moving up to the old Ivory soap, "99-44/100% pure," standard? Is a statistical improvement of .54 percent significant? Depends on your point of view. Using the Ivory standard, only 375 surgical patients a day would now suffer our acceptable "realistic performance shortfall." That's definitely an improvement, but it still adds up to an annual total of 112,560 surgical groaners and goners. Again, not that good.

How about if we go way out on the quality limb here and set our ambitious but attainable standard at 99.9 percent?

*Zero defections is a registered trademark of Bain & Company.

Would that be good enough? In a 1991 Special Report on Quality in *TRAINING* magazine, Natalie Gabel applied that standard to a variety of everyday activities. The numbers she came up with are startling. If 99.9 percent were the actual performance standard attained by some everyday organizations:

- The IRS would lose 2 million documents this year.
- Film producers would ship out 811,000 faulty rolls of 35mm film for capturing your precious moments.
- Hospital nurseries would give 12 babies to the wrong parents—each day.
- The U.S. Post Office would mishandle 18,322 pieces of mail—every hour.
- Financial institutions would deduct 22,000 checks from the wrong bank accounts—in the next 60 minutes.
- Telecommunication services would misplace 1,314 phone calls—in the next 60 seconds.

In the next 12 months:

- 268,500 defective tires would be rolled out.
- 103,260 income tax returns would be processed incorrectly.
- 5,517,200 cases of soft drinks would be flatter than a bad tire.
- 55 malfunctioning ATMs would be installed.
- 20,000 incorrect drug prescriptions would be written.
- 114,500 mismatched pairs of shoes would trip up unwary consumers.
- $761,900 would be spent on tapes and CDs that won't play.

Had enough? According to Gabel, that's the good news. She also turned up entire industries where the idea of 99.9 percent is a goodly distance over the horizon. When Hewlett-Packard checked out 300,000 semiconductors from three American and three Japanese firms recently, it found the average failure rate of the American chips was more than 0.1 percent.

Think that's good? The failure rate for the Japanese chips in the same time period was *zero*.

Despite millions of dollars of advertising about improved performance, Gabel discovered the U.S. airline industry's own figures reporting that just 80 percent of domestic flights left at their scheduled and advertised times, and only 74 percent arrived at their destinations on schedule. U.S. flag carriers also assumed that 5–10 percent of all baggage would routinely be mishandled and 3 percent of all checked baggage just plain lost en route.

And don't look to the heavens for succor. According to Gabel, the Office of Technology Assessment reports that of the more than 20,000 objects fired into earth orbit since 1975, fewer than 5 percent remain operational.

Good Numbers

On the bright side of the service quality percentage game, actual records show that of those 67,000 daily surgical patients we noted earlier, only 25 will fail to pull through today. That's 0.000037, or 0.037 percent, or a success rate of 99.963 percent, 15 times better than the 99.9 percent standard. Not Six Sigma, but not bad, either. *Six Sigma,* by the way, is a term used by Motorola, which credited winning the 1989 Malcolm Baldrige National Quality Award to its quality improvement process of that name. As a measurement, Sigma refers to quality defects per million parts. A Six Sigma standard permits only 3.4 defects per million, an incredibly high level of quality compared to Five Sigma (233 defects per million) and Four Sigma (6,210 defects per million). To put that in the context of the 99 percent scale, a company with one defect per 100 will count 10,000 defects per million.

In the real world, according to the Gannett News Service, the airlines actually outperform many of the world's best manufacturers when it comes to safety. Counting fatalities as defects, they would achieve a level of 6.5 Sigma. Alas, on baggage handling, the news is less upbeat: 3.5 Sigma. By comparison,

doctors and pharmacists score Five Sigma when it comes to
accuracy in writing and filling prescriptions.

But put away the calculator. You don't need to solve for X
in the service quality equation because the only "acceptable
quality level" is 100 percent. That's the only number customers
will really accept. (If you doubt it, ask them sometime how
many times out of 100, or 1,000, you can drive their car into
the oil pit, or put their daughter's braces in wrong, or substitute three-day-old pizza for one fresh out of the oven.) It is
indeed possible to make a tough service quality standard a
realistic goal. And it's increasingly becoming a good idea.

Customers can tell the difference.

Good is not good where better is expected.

—Thomas Fuller
British author

6

Listening Is a Contact Sport

"Just listening doesn't get you much these days. You've got to help customers feel the impact of your listening."

—David H. Radack
Vice President,
Amdahl, Inc., Sunnyvale, California

Listening well is a rarity in our society. That helps explain the popularity of psychologists, the scale of the divorce rate, and why there are so many self-help books with communications as their central theme. As a manager, you have to serve as both listening post and traffic analyst. Neither is as simple as it sounds.

Part of the challenge of listening is filtering out the noise of bias and defensiveness. When your frontline workers hear customers suggesting ways your business could do more for them, the instinctive response is to determine how much additional work that might mean. When they hear negative comments from customers about their or the organization's service performance, they have a natural tendency to defend and protect.

Their inherent sense of "possessiveness" about the delivery system and their tendency to take complaints as a personal attack make it harder for people at the front line to listen in a nonjudgmental way. Although your people are up close and personal with customers on a day-to-day basis, you are actually in a better position to listen effectively. As a manager, one step removed, you should have less defensiveness and a broader frame of reference than the immediate moment.

Additionally, frontline workers typically listen to customers for cues on what to do in what order, instructions for tasks to be completed, or requests for problems to be solved. The "immediate action required" nature of this exchange makes it difficult—though not impossible—to spot themes and trends and patterns at the front line. As a manager, you're more likely to have a forestwide perspective than a tree-by-tree view.

Listen, Understand, Respond

Listening does not mean simply looking at someone while they talk and then doing something in response. There's an important middle piece to the puzzle: Listening means actively seeking to understand another person. That's why we say it's a contact sport. Listening without contact, listening without dramatic connection, is like looking without seeing. Given the uniqueness of being *really* heard, customers remember long those who listen well.

It's also important to listen to the things your frontline people can tell you about constantly changing customer needs and expectations. In settings from Walt Disney World to the regional answering centers of American Express, customer contact people debrief each other periodically to spot new problems or requests, emerging opportunities, and the influence of larger market conditions. When managers act on their information, the message comes through loud and clear: Pay attention to your customers. We're interested in what they're telling you. That's how we learn to serve them better.

Make sure you don't listen to one source of information at the expense of another one. Marketing professor Leonard Berry of Texas A&M University tells the story of a new manager at the Chicago Marriott. One day, while going over year-end budget requests, he came across a $20,000 line item to upgrade the black-and-white television sets to color in the bathrooms of the rooms on the concierge level. At first glance, it seemed like a nice enough service improvement. But something teased at the edge of his service vision.

So the manager started asking questions of his people, based in part on the implicit assumption that they had been listening to customers and hence would have a good handle on guest preferences and requests. First, he asked the concierge level staff and the people in engineering how many requests they had received for color sets in the bathrooms on that level. "Actually, none," came the reply, "but we thought it was a neat idea."

Then he asked the housekeeping staff assigned to the concierge level what they were hearing from guests on the floor—what was the most requested item that they didn't have. Their reply: irons and ironing boards. Guess what he authorized for purchase under that line item? And as an unexpected reward for listening, *understanding*, and responding, it turned out that the cost of putting in irons and ironing boards was less than the cost of upgrading black-and-white television sets to color.

Seven Ways to Listen for Consumer Needs and Expectations

There are lots of ways to listen—and to listen well, you need to master and use more than one style. It's like using a belt and suspenders to hold up your pants. The redundant systems reinforce each other, but they do so in different styles with different strengths and weaknesses. Consider the following.

1. *Face-to-face.* More and more managers are uncomfortable with the idea that the information they are getting is indirect. They want to know things directly and personally. Erie "Chip" Chapman, III, CEO of U.S. Health Corporation, the regional holding company that numbers Riverside Methodist Hospital in Columbus, Ohio, as its crown jewel, is a good example. Chapman routinely spends one day a week on the front lines, often wearing a volunteer's anonymous coat to

reduce the odds that people will slant what they're saying because they know who's listening. Interestingly, he says the customer he's listening to isn't just the patient. He listens to his people, too. His reasoning is simple: His personal customer isn't the patient, it's his people, because those people treat the patients, he doesn't.

2. *Comment and complaint analysis.* Some customers will tell you what's on their mind face-to-face. Some won't risk the chance of confrontation or embarrassment, but will fill out simple "Tell Us, Rate Us, Help Us" comment cards. Tracking them can give you a continuing barometric reading on how you're doing. More extensive contacts, such as complaint and compliment letters, can be mined for detailed insights into past experiences and future preferences.

As an aside, use what you hear, not only for your own purposes, but to reward customers for their initiative in providing the information as well as people in your organization who have distinguished themselves in the customer's eyes. Within twenty-four to forty-eight hours, every comment, complaint, or suggestion (100 *a day* is average) dropped into the box at the front of Stew Leonard's Dairy Store in Norwalk, Connecticut, is acknowledged, by phone and then in writing, to let customers know somebody cares. Companies such as Precision LensCrafters, Amica Mutual Insurance, Delta Air Lines, Southern Bell, and Federal Express make sure customer kudos are used to reward and reinforce their people for a job well done.

3. *Customer hotlines.* Make it easy to listen by making it easy for the customer to talk to you. Riverside Methodist offers out-of-town physicians a twenty-four-hour toll-free line so they can check on patients they've referred to the hospital. Procter & Gamble not only uses 800 numbers for customer inquiries, suggestions and complaints, but it segments them to reflect product types. CompuServe, Basy's, and other computer services firms maintain modem-accessed "bulletin boards" as customer forums, allowing them to listen electronically, too.

4. *Frontline contacts.* Employees who know what to listen for hear plenty in their day-to-day dealings with customers.

Federal Express drivers are trained to look and listen for competitors as a clue to new services the company can supply.
Stew Leonard's Dairy Store periodically loads up a van with
half a dozen managers, cashiers, and stockers and drops by a
competitor, where each is assigned the task of finding something—good, bad, or indifferent—the business can learn from.

5. *Customer advisory panels.* Your best customers, the ones
who have been with you for years, represent not only a valued
relationship, but a source of savvy insight into your service
operations. Use them like a board of directors for the front line.
Your worst can also be an asset when you find active ways to
listen. Emerald Peoples Utility District, a small public power
co-op based in Eugene, Oregon, gets customers involved in
various committees and study groups. Arizona Public Service,
a much larger regional utility based in Phoenix, has recruited
some of the public interest advocates who once dogged its
every step to bring their interest and energy inside the walls,
where they can be applied in useful ways.

6. *Mutual education.* The more your customers know about
doing business with you, the more they can help you find
better ways to serve them. Companies from multinational 3M
to Quad/Graphics, a commercial printer based in the Milwaukee suburb of Pewaukee, bring customers to company facilities—or take training to the customer's site—working hard to
explain technical processes, quality techniques, custom options, and new wrinkles. Customers see the chance to go to
camp with a valued vendor as a way to make sure they get
their money's worth from the services they buy. From the
provider standpoint, the extended contacts give service and
quality staffers a chance to mine their customers for new
insights.

7. *Formal research.* Last, but certainly not least, there's the
traditional spectrum of proven techniques for data collection.
Mail-in and live surveys, focus groups, telemarketing contacts,
mystery shopping services, demographic analysis, and random sampling of target audiences help shade in the various
colors of the big picture. Domino's, Shoney's restaurants, Jiffy
Lube oil-change centers, and a growing number of automobile

manufacturers and dealers even find ways to listen to themselves being customers, sending their own service quality investigators (some of them recruited from among the ranks of customers) unannounced to every location in their respective systems. (We look at formal research in more detail in Chapter 18.)

> Listening is useless unless it creates actions which realign efforts based on what is learned.
>
> —Fred Smith
> Founder and chairman, Federal Express

7

A Complaining Customer Is Your Best Friend

One of the surest signs of a bad or declining relationship with a customer is the absence of complaints. Nobody is ever that satisfied, especially not over an extended period of time. The customer is either not being candid or not being contacted.

—Theodore Levitt
Harvard University

Wait a minute! Weren't we just promoting zero defections and 100 percent quality? Aren't we supposed to be working to make sure absolutely everything goes absolutely right absolutely every time the customer comes in contact with us?

Absolutely.

But the fact of the matter is, it won't. Inevitably, things can and will go wrong over the course of a service relationship. And when they do, you want to know about it, and the sooner the better. At least, you do if you're sincerely interested in building a long-term relationship that's strong enough to weather the occasional goof or glitch.

In a way, observes Harvard marketing professor Theodore Levitt, a quality customer relationship is like a marriage. "The sale consummates the courtship," he writes, "at which point the marriage begins. The quality of the 'marriage' depends on how well the seller manages the relationship."

Just as personal relationships have their occasional rough spots, so, too, will a customer relationship have its ups and downs. If there's real long-term value in the relationship, both parties will have an incentive to overcome the periodic problems and, through the process of doing so, make the relationship even stronger. In contrast, an absence of candor that causes one partner to gloss over or fail to mention problems reflects declining trust and a deteriorating relationship.

A strong, enduring customer service relationship will be founded on clear, open communications—whether the matter at hand is good or bad. Customers who take the time to bring their problems to us or offer advice on how we can get better at meeting their needs are customers who believe we care enough to act on their complaints, not just feel good about their compliments. They're telling us they still see value in the relationship continuing—if, that is, things can get back to a sound and mutually satisfying level. They're really a golden asset.

By contrast, avoiding complaints, pretending that everything is "just peachy" (even when you know it isn't), pretending to assertively solicit customer feedback with one hand while backhanding the customer for daring to utter a discouraging word with the other are sure signs that the relationship has not achieved enough maturity to weather the candor. That way lies dissolution. And since the customer always gets custody of the business they can bring to a relationship, you'll not only have to replace them, you'll also have to watch them take up with your bitterest rivals: your competition.

Stimulating Complaints

TARP, the Technical Assistance Research Programs Institute, a Washington, DC–based customer service research organization, provides a detailed picture of customer complaints and their effects on customer/company relationships. According to TARP's continuing studies, about a quarter of the typical business's customers are dissatisfied enough to switch to a competitor at any given time.

- ▲ Yet the average business only receives complaints from about 4 percent of its disgruntled customers. An amazing 96 percent of unhappy customers—and 99 out of 100 people in the total customer base—will suffer in silence. They'd rather switch than fight.

How can that be? Well, why does an upset diner usually answer "fine" if asked how everything was, when, in fact, the meal and/or the service were a disappointment? Why do people often wear clothes and shoes that are half a size too large or too small rather than return them to the store for a replacement that fits better? Why don't people just level with us? Don't they know how much we want and need their feedback today?

In point of fact, no, they don't know. There are three basic reasons why customers choose to vote with their feet and go looking for another service provider rather than stick around and try to work the problem through with us:

1. They don't think we care.
2. They don't have any hope—they don't think anything good is going to happen, even if we do care.
3. They don't have any courage—experience has taught them that "no good turn goes unpunished," leading them to fear that the service provider will find a way to retaliate against them the next time.

Though customers are not inclined to tell us, it's worth noting that they will tell plenty of other people: fourteen to twenty of them on average when they're dissatisfied. Comparatively speaking, truly satisfied customers will tell just five to seven people about a service provider who really dazzled them. And what do researchers consistently find to be the most powerful and persuasive form of advertising? You guessed it—word of mouth.

Warts and All

Over the years, American business has done a pretty fair job of convincing customers to suffer in silence. Now, when we want, need, and are beginning to respect the value of this kind of informed feedback, we have to literally coax customers to provide it. There are a lot of reasons for this state of affairs:

- In some cases, we've lulled ourselves into thinking "no news is good news," or that it's better to "let sleeping dogs lie."
- Sometimes we fear that if we seek and receive customer complaints, and no corrective action ensues, we might be perceived in a worse light than if we'd left well enough alone. Research, however, contradicts that assumption: Better to have asked and not acted, it finds, than not to have asked at all.
- In some cases, we simply haven't figured out how effectively to ask for complaints without sounding almost masochistic: "Please, tell us how bad we are."
- Some of us have asked incorrectly, making the process of registering a complaint so convoluted or obviously pointless that we fail to get helpful information.
- And some of us have simply given up asking, often because it wasn't an organizational imperative.

All this is changing. And high time it did. The TARP studies offer an interesting perspective on the costs of soliciting complaints and the rewards for acting on them. When the amount involved is in excess of $100, customers who don't complain at all have about a 37 percent likelihood of doing business with us again. If they complain and it's like talking to the proverbial brick wall, the odds of them coming back nonetheless go up to about fifty-fifty.

If they complain and we do nothing more than listen to them, the chances that they will come back again go up to about 70 percent. And when we listen and *respond to them*, even when the complaint isn't resolved in their favor, TARP's research shows that the chances of them giving us another chance are about 95 percent. By comparison, customers who pronounce themselves "satisfied" come back about 90 percent of the time.

- ▲ In other words, complaining customers who are properly handled can become even more loyal than customers who have never had a problem.

How to Make Complaining Easier

Complaining customers are important, in and of themselves. Their relationship with us is in obvious jeopardy and needs to be returned to a positive state. Complaining customers also are important because, statistically speaking, they represent other dissatisfied customers who are convinced that there's no point in telling us about their bad experiences with us. These custom- ers are saying, "Please don't throw us away. We want the opportunity to be your customer again." Following are some tactics to help you get the most from those encounters.

1. *When you have an opportunity to address a complainant face-to-face, listen.* Work consciously at graciousness and control. Avoid becoming defensive or acting stern and cold or judgmen- tal. Especially avoid attempting to explain why the problem occurred. When they are levying complaints, customers are not particularly interested in your explanations for poor ser- vice, let alone what *they* should have done differently. They want to know: (1) that they are being heard, and (2) that their comments are valued. Your explanations of why things work the way they do will be seen as defensive and will only aggravate and irritate.

2. *Treat complaints about your customer contact people as an opportunity.* Use them for problem-solving and learning, not for rebuke and judgment. If you punish your frontline people when they bring you customer complaints or feedback, they will find ways to keep future feedback from you. Keep in mind

that the customer is *not* always right. Research shows that about 30 percent of all service problems are actually caused by the customer. The objective isn't to assign blame and hand out punishment. It's to find out what happened, why, what you can do to resolve it this time, and what you can do to prevent it from happening again.

3. *Be assertive in soliciting customer feedback.* Nothing you or your people are doing is more important than taking care of customers. That process doesn't end with ringing up a sale. Stimulate the dialogue with words like "We are really anxious to do all we can to improve our service, and your feedback would be very helpful." Don't shut the door on additional details, either. When they've gotten through the key points of the story, probe for helpful details and other ideas: "Thanks, that helps a lot. What else could we do to improve our service?"

4. *Encourage your frontline people to ask for feedback.* Make it clear by words and actions that you think customers can help you build rewarding, long-term, profitable relationships that benefit everyone involved. Be a good role model by asking customers for feedback in the presence of your frontline staff. Listen, understand, and respond to what your staffers have been hearing so they know that you'll act on what they can tell you.

5. *Use negative feedback to improve performance, not punish people.* When you get complaints from customers regarding your people, thank the customer involved for the information and make it clear that you will check into the problem, but without either scapegoating your employees or "shooting the messenger" by defending your people on general principles. Then, when you meet with your frontline person, present the feedback, not in a blaming or judgmental way, but with a descriptive "Let's figure out what we can do to resolve this situation" type of approach.

6. *Don't take sides.* If you find yourself in the line of fire between the customer and your employee, take the high ground. Instead of choosing sides, your best approach will be to try to collect facts and make a decision based on the *perform-ance*, not the *people* involved. Remember that win-lose situations

leave losers (and negative feelings) in their aftermath. The balance you have to achieve is between reaffirming the customer for complaining and reinforcing your people so they'll continue to have the confidence to deal with customers.

> Just because you don't think it's a big deal doesn't mean your customer doesn't think it's a big deal. When your customer *says* it's a big deal, it's a big deal. And when your customer says, "It's *no* big deal," it's *still* a big deal. Otherwise, why would they bring it up?
>
> —Kristin Anderson
> Performance Research Associates

8

Little Things Mean a Lot

It's not the one thousand dollar things that upset the customer, but the five buck things that bug them.

—Earl Fletcher
Sales and management trainer,
Volkswagen Canada

New arrivals to the combat zones of Vietnam quickly learned that the difference between a veteran and a novice was far more than war stories. They had an expression for it on the front lines: "grunt eyes." Grunts were the enlisted ranks of the infantry—low rank, little prestige, people whose job description started and ended with the simple requirement, "Do what the 'old man' tells you to do."

Those with "grunt eyes" were able to see things a new in-country recruit would completely miss. And there was little correlation with rank. Whether you were a captain or a private, you only acquired "grunt eyes" in the field, paying attention to every sight, sound, smell, impulse, clue, and condition that often could make the difference between life and death. It was something learned, not something taught. The common skeptic's question, immortalized in the movie *Full Metal Jacket*, was "I see you talk the talk, but do you walk the walk?"

As a manager, you've no doubt learned a fair amount of service talk in recent years. But have you also learned the service walk? Have you developed "grunt eyes" attuned to your own frontline conditions? Do you really notice and understand the subtleties of what you see? The survival of your business is riding on it. According to our survey research, about 22 percent of the difference between satisfied and dissatisfied customers can be accounted for by an organization's ability to recognize and manage the details that really matter for customers.

Attention to details is a prime characteristic of Knock Your Socks Off Service.

Fred Smith, founder and chairman of Federal Express, begins many of his visits in various FedEx cities by hopping into a delivery van and riding with a driver to see his operations where they most affect the customer.

Bill Marriott, chairman of the hotel chain that bears the family name, often takes a turn at the front desk checking in guests. If he sees a dirty ashtray in the lobby, he empties it. If there's trash in the parking lot, he picks it up.

• Similarly, grunt-eyed managers and frontliners alike at Walt Disney World and Disneyland, McDonald's, and Delta Air Lines, and thousands of other dedicated businesses pick up trash, polish counters, straighten displays, spruce up plants, and worry over the 101 details that together combine to make their customers' experiences with them memorable for all the right reasons.

But attention to details involves more than just playing janitor so your people will know they should imitate your concern for what the customer sees. It also means remembering that details are at the heart of the Moments of Truth—those moments when the customer is in contact with your organization and forms an opinion of the quality of what you do. Manage the Moments of Truth well and you earn an A or a B on their highly subjective report cards. Ignore them, or manage them poorly, and customers give you a D or an F. Then they start looking for someone more likely to make the grade.

The Service Walk

As a manager, how can you hope to figure out which of the thousands of possible Moments of Truth customers can experience with your organization are the ones that need to be handled to perfection? Traditional measurement and analysis can help: both the large-scale kind, such as market research and detailed customer surveys, and more anecdotal and fragmented forms, like customer comment cards, letters, phone calls, and impromptu conversations with customers you meet on and off the job.

It's not the details in and of themselves that are important—it's the relative importance attached to them by the customer. In other words, before you make your people crazy by mandating that phones will be answered within two rings, or three rings, or eight rings, make sure your customers consider that an important service quality factor. View other details from the customer's standpoint as well. It will save you a lot of headaches and heartaches.

A few years ago, John Barrier, in Spokane, Washington, asked a bank receptionist to validate his parking slip after he'd cashed a check. With a glance at his dirty construction clothes, the receptionist informed him that he hadn't conducted a real "transaction" and suggested he make a deposit. The branch manager also refused to stamp the parking ticket (the value involved was sixty cents). So Barrier called the bank's headquarters in Spokane and vowed to withdraw all of his deposits unless the manager apologized. No call came. The next day, he came back—and withdrew $1 million. And the next day as well. The bank lost a customer with more than $2 million on deposit over a sixty-cent parking voucher.

Defining the details in general is only a starting point. You can't manage service in absentia. You need to develop your own "grunt eyes" when it comes to service, making sure you walk the walk as well as talk the talk.

To take the "service walk," start by determining how your services look to your customers based on their prepurchase expectations. When you enter a bank or a car repair shop, a theater or a fast-food restaurant, a doctor's office or an airplane, you have some notion of what ought to occur. The first thing you do is compare what's actually happening to that expectation. And when it doesn't match up, you can find yourself disoriented and confused—whether because you're dismayed or dazzled.

- If you walked into a Hardee's or McDonald's and found candles and fine china on the tables, with waiters in tuxedos hovering nearby, you'd think you were in the wrong place.
- By the same token, if you arrived for dinner at five-star Chez Ritzy and encountered the standard Hardee's or McDonald's decor, menu, and service style, you would also wonder what was afoot.

From that starting point, service quality becomes a function of experience—what happens to you as the customer. Service transactions are actually a succession of individual Moments of Truth—in essence, a trail of experiences with specific steps from start to finish. Each step is important, but some have more weight than others. And individual customers will change the relative weighting in keeping with their own likes and dislikes.

That's why it's so important to see and evaluate your services the way your customers do. The math involved is relatively simple. If the experience matches their expectations, they'll judge it to be satisfactory, though hardly memorable. When it turns out differently than they expected, it becomes more memorable precisely because of its lower or higher than expected quality.

Two factors are considered by the customer: process and outcome—what they experience and what they get. Both must match expectations for service to be judged satisfactory; both must exceed expectations for service to be viewed as superior. But if either is substandard, the customer's combined rating will drop off the bottom of the charts.

- When the meal (outcome) is wonderful, but you have to go through hell (process) to get it, the net score will be negative.
- Likewise, even when you're treated like a king by the car repair shop (process), if your car still doesn't work prop-

erly (outcome), the net score is negative. In other words, an incompetent physical administered by a dead ringer for kindly young Dr. Kildare will not satisfy. But neither will a competent physical administered by a brusque, arrogant physician—or one who hasn't bathed since the last full moon. The caring is as important as the care to winning the customer's loyalty. You have to do both to succeed.

Dealing with Details

Many organizations put a great deal of time and energy into managing and monitoring the service outcome—the check was cashed, the operation was completed, the account was closed. Outcomes, by and large, are easy to define and count. But paying attention to all the little details involved in the service process is a lot tougher. It's difficult to identify and define, let alone measure and evaluate, everything the customer has to go through to get to that outcome. But that's what you, and everyone working with and for you, must learn to do as part of your service walk.

To see just how detailed your customer-level journey can be, consider the variables involved only at the points where a customer might enter your delivery system.

If it's a parking lot—is it easy to access, well lit, clearly marked, safe to use? Are the parking lot's users (customers) favored over the parking lot's owners (your people, especially internal VIPs)? Is it clear from wherever the customers have to park which door should be entered? Ask yourself, "If the customer's experience in the parking lot were a picture of our whole service system, what would it tell them about what we value, how we feel about customers, where our priorities lie?"

If it's an admitting office, a reception area, a security check-in—how is the area kept? Is it comfortable, clean, user-friendly? Is it easy for customers to figure out where to go, who to see, what to do? Are there resources, aids, supports, and guides if the customer gets confused, bored, or lost? Are such materials current and professional, or does their age qualify them as museum pieces? What is done to manage wait time? What would a picture of this scene tell the customer about the rest of the service delivery systems they'll shortly be encountering?

If it involves objects, forms, systems, or procedures—are they clearly written, professionally produced, truly necessary? Will they be perceived as user-friendly, customer-focused, an aid to making you easy to do business with? Do they work properly, and the first time? Can they be understood by the customer without the aid of a dictionary, an interpreter, or an internal expert?

If the customer enters your service delivery system by phone—is the system large enough and sophisticated enough to handle the load, easy to understand and use, efficient and time-effective? Is the phone answered quickly, and by a person enthusiastically and obviously anxious to assist? Must your customers negotiate their way through a long and involved voicemail system made up of seemingly endless menus of buttons to push before encountering a live human voice? Are phone encounters rushed to meet an artificial time standard? Or prolonged well beyond the time the customer has allotted for your assistance? If the customer must be transferred, how will it feel and sound on their end of the line? What do they experience when they're put on hold—silence, elevator music, boring advertisements, long waits?

Service Patrols

The service walk can be taken solo, but it's an equally valid tactic as something you do with one or several of your frontline people. From time to time, ask some of *them* to join you in trying on the customer's clodhoppers. Let them tell you what they see when they use their own "grunt eyes" to reexamine aspects of the service delivery system and experience that have become taken for granted over time. Ask them to point out weak spots, bottlenecks, points of both pride and embarrassment, and areas for improvement identified by customers and their own firsthand knowledge of what is involved in taking care of business.

The more you encourage frontline people to see themselves as responsible for the service experience—and the systems that make those experiences successful or difficult—the more willing and empowered they will feel to truly take care of their customers.

Jan Carlzon, the architect of the service turnaround at Scandinavian Airline Systems (SAS) in the early 1980s, once summarized the journey from hip-deep red ink to basic black on the bottom line as a matter of details, details, details: "We never started out to become 1,000 percent better at anything; just 1 percent better at a thousand different things that are important to the customer—and it worked."

But at SAS, just as at Disney, Marriott, Federal Express, and countless other outstanding service providers, managers continue to not only talk the talk, but walk the walk.

> You don't improve service and quality in general. You improve service and quality in specific.
>
> —Dr. Rodney Dueck
> Park Nicollet Medical Centers, Minneapolis

9

Building Service Partnerships

When management fails to understand customer desires for the service, a chain reaction of mistakes is likely to follow. The wrong service standards. The wrong training. The wrong types of performance measurements. The wrong advertising. And so forth. It is tough enough to satisfy customer desires without the added burden of not really knowing what desires to satisfy.

—Leonard Berry, David Bennet, Carter Brown
Service Quality

Traditionally, service partnerships have been associated with the sale of big ticket items: mainframe computers, a fleet of company autos, raw material for a steel mill. They've also been common to big ticket professional services, particularly those provided by law, CPA, advertising, engineering, and consulting firms.

Although the concept of service partnership generally implies a long-standing relationship, the "feeling of partnership" may be created in the short term as well. It is founded on a form of unconditional serving in which the service provider consciously overlooks the short-term cost to lay the foundation of a long-term relationship.

Nurturing service relationships into service partnerships is a primary ingredient in the Nordstrom-Federal Express-LensCrafters approach to service quality that consistently turns satisfied customers into friends, partners, and walking testimonials. The evidence can be seen in such customer comments as "I can count on them to work with me," "I've tried others, but no one knows me as well, so I keep coming back," or "Whenever I run into problems, they always help me find a solution."

Many businesses build partnerships into the very philosophy of their customer/client relationships:

- AMP, an international electronics components manufacturer headquartered in Harrisburg, Pennsylvania, focuses on "early involvement"—working partnerships through which it develops tooling and procedures in association with the client companies that will be using its plugs and connectors.
- When 3M Company scientists invented S-VHS videotape, no VCR existed that could get the optimum performance available in the product. Since 3M doesn't make videocassette recorders, it took its ideas and invention to a company that did: Japan-based JVC, holder of the original patents on VHS technology.
- To "reality check" the design and services to be built into the new Elizabeth Blackwell Center, a two-floor enclave dedicated to women's health needs, Riverside Methodist Hospital conducted interviews and focus groups with more than 500 women in the Columbus, Ohio, area.

Two caveats about partnerships:

1. All partnerships, whether they involve a colleague, a customer, or a spouse, require a more complete and deeper commitment. They have more stringent requirements. They take more work than a transient contact or temporary service relationship. And they must be mutually beneficial and desirable to work.
2. Not all customers want to participate in service partnerships. Some, for example, enjoy a certain amount of mystery and privacy. As the service relationship becomes more intense and intimate, they back off and

switch to another service relationship (often with exit language that says such things as "They knew us too well" or "We needed some breathing room"). Other customers desire the "serve me" relationship, enjoying the deference of the service provider and preferring to make no reciprocal investment on their part.

Given all that, are service partnerships worth the extra effort they require? You bet! Not only are service partnerships more economically rewarding, they can endure more mistakes, will be more forgiving over time, and will produce greater intrinsic payoffs than traditional transaction-based provider-to-customer encounters.

Principles of Partnership

The easiest way to see what makes a service partnership work is to look at it under duress—in those moments when the relationship is most vulnerable. A service partnership is "at risk" at three turns:

1. When the relationship is beginning, or during the "dating stage" when it begins to solidify (*alignment*).
2. When an error or failure has occurred to challenge it (*blunders*).
3. When there is a change impacting the relationship such as new competition, technological developments, alterations in the economy, or reorganization of the service provider's or the customer's company (*change*).

Let's see how to manage your service partnerships during these three stages.

During Alignment

1. Partnerships begin with a clear, mutual focus on needs to be met. Just as young people have to learn unselfishness in order to transform "one-night stand" dating experiences into

longer term relationships, service providers must make sure that greed does not dominate service delivery at this stage. The economic rewards of good service must be available, of course, but if the service focus lacks a large dose of mutuality, the relationship will lack substance and be short-lived.

Chicago-based Baxter Healthcare willingly shares its corporate resources and expertise on everything from hazardous waste disposal to its internal quality process. Baxter maintains a staff of fifty quality professionals who conduct training, provide consulting, and assist with quality efforts both within Baxter and with some 200 hospitals and other healthcare providers nationwide.

2. Partnerships work best when they are collaborative. Collaborative comes from a Latin word meaning "to work together." The typical service relationship puts the service provider in a deferent role—"We'll do whatever it takes to make you happy, Mr./Ms. Customer." That kind of reactive deference and the mutual exchange of a viable partnership are impossible bedfellows. The customer is also responsible for helping the relationship to grow.

3. Partnerships are relationships between people before they are contracts between units or organizations. A frequent flyer accompanied by his wife, who was flying on a free ticket, sought to get the two of them a first-class upgrade. The gate attendant tersely quoted the rule forbidding upgrade coupons from being used with frequent flyer tickets. "Look," said the frustrated passenger, "your plane is practically empty, we leave in ten minutes, there are no passengers in first class, and I fly enough miles with your airline to get a free jet plane." "I'm sorry, sir," said the agent, "but we have our rules." The now angry customer replied, "Yeah, you *do* have your rules." He paused for a few seconds, then added, "And one less frequent flyer!"

During Blunders

1. Partners are not afraid to ask for feedback or to say "I'm sorry." "Fix the customer, then the customer's problem" is an axiom that sets the proper priorities when services break down.

Unlike a faulty product, which becomes the object of anger when it ceases to function properly, when services fail to satisfy, the customer is apt to feel personally affronted. Correction begins with healing the relationship, usually starting with a heartfelt "I'm sorry" (as opposed to "We're sorry).

2. Partnerships are psychological, not rational/logical, when blunders threaten. One outgrowth of the production era of yesteryear was the belief that all problems could be corrected through science and technology. Yet, as one ad for "volunteers for disaster assistance" aptly stated, "Machines can rebuild a broken bridge and science can repair a broken arm, but only another human can mend a broken heart." At the core of blunder management is a person-to-person reconnection, an empathetic response that attempts to fix the partnership itself.

3. Partnerships anticipate that things will go wrong. Murphy's Law is axiomatic in service. Both the customer and the service provider know it. Consequently, effective service partnerships include in their frequent dialogue a discussion of what might someday go wrong and how both parties would like it handled if it ever does.

The Plaza Club—the top two concierge floors of the Radisson at Mark Plaza in Alexandria, Virginia—prides itself on repeat guests. Once a guest has become "a regular," concierge Penny Spinney makes a point of discussing what they would like the hotel to do if they ever call for a reservation and find the Club booked up for one or more nights of a particular stay. Together, they explore options such as putting the guest on a floor just below the Club while offering full lounge privileges, thus laying the groundwork for turning a potential disappointment into a smooth and satisfying repeat visit.

During Change

1. Partnerships work when partners plan how they will deal with nonalignment. Every partnership encounters strains provoked by change. Sometimes it's deliberate: price changes, expansion, consolidation, reorganization, acquisition; sometimes a result of unintentional or competitive pressures, hostile takeovers, a general economic downturn, or other factors. Just

as partners in a strong marriage anticipate changes and plan ways to deal with the occasional "out of sync" condition, so, too, must those in service partnership.

Jack Sherwood, author and consultant, observes that the secret to long-term relationships enduring disruptive change is that "both parties agree that whenever either party senses the possibility of an impending disruption, the feeling is shared and the possibility of renegotiation is raised." Too often, partners holding to the "see no evil" approach ignore intuitive signals of a problem in the making. By the time they acknowledge the situation, negative feelings turn what could have been a calm conversation into a wrangle, or the relationship limps along in silence until it dies from neglect.

2. Partnerships are based on honesty and openness, not on phony agreement. Honesty and openness are a continuation of the planned renegotiation theme. When researchers at the Battelle Memorial Institute in Columbus, Ohio, undertake a research project for a client, they know—and they explain to the client—that the research effort might not prove out. While the work is in progress, Battelle engineers make sure their clients receive regular updates, no matter how well or how disappointingly things are going. No news isn't good news.

3. Partnerships remember to celebrate their partnership. One of the biggest culprits in the failure of marriages is the absence of spirit—when the romance fades, so, too, does the relationship. Service partnerships need spirit to keep the excitement and emotional connection. Celebration can be a way to communicate that the relationship is not taken for granted. It can be a way to rekindle that feeling of excitement that characterized the relationship during its formative stage.

> As a result of our working with these hospitals on quality issues, we've come to know each other better in general. We can work more comfortably on joint problems.
>
> —David Auld,
> Vice President, Quality Leadership, Baxter Healthcare

Imperative 3
Focus on "Purpose"

Yogi Berra, the immortal New York Yankee catcher and coach, is supposed to have said, "If you don't know where you're going, you're liable to end up someplace else." It's true—whether he said it or not. It is especially true of your efforts to create Knock Your Socks Off Service. Your vision of what superior service looks like is the foundation of getting where you want to go. And not "someplace else."

Focusing on *purpose* means articulating that vision for the people who work with you. What it will take to cause customers to give you a five-star rating may be very clear in *your* mind. That is of little consequence until everyone charged with turning that vision into reality for the customer sees that vision just as clearly as you see it.

That vision—we refer to it as a "service strategy statement"—must be personally meaningful and important to everyone in the organization if it is going to become reality for the customer. That means it must not only be understandable, it must also be measurable. Concrete standards of service quality make the vision real and palpable; regular and extensive measurement makes it meaningful.

Vision without action is dreaming. Action without vision is random activity. Vision and action together can change the world.

—Joel Barker
Futurist

10

The Power of Purpose

If you don't know where you are going, any road will take you there.

—David Campbell
Industrial psychologist

A cattle rancher will tell you that moving a large herd requires bifocal vision: without close attention to the herd, a feisty steer can double back or break away, making the rancher waste important time retrieving the malcontent. But if you don't also keep an eye on the distant gate—your ultimate destination—you may never get there.

When it comes to Knock Your Socks Off Service, focusing on the ultimate as well as the immediate is equally critical. "Bifocal" service vision comes from a clear focus on purpose: Defining in detail and in writing—and then repeating constantly and consistently—what your organization means when it says "Quality customer service is our goal." Your focus on purpose—your "service strategy statement"—is your tool for aligning the day-to-day actions of your employees with the distant gate of Knock Your Socks Off Service.

Your organization probably has a mission statement. Perhaps a vision statement as well. That's great. But to keep your unit focus sharp, you need your *own* well-defined, carefully worded service strategy statement. Your statement may be unique to your unit or a variation on the organization's central strategy. It should say who your customers are, what you do that is of value to them, and how you—and they—will know it when you—and they—see it.

Defining what you are trying to ultimately accomplish with and for customers helps your people understand the rhyme and reason of the work they do. Your strategy statement should be so well defined that your people always know which side to come down on when they face decisions about how to provide truly superior service. It's not magic. It's simply the power of purpose.

Your service strategy statement, when done well, will:

- Ensure that everyone in your unit is working with the same idea of "what's important around here."
- Provide employees far removed from the power centers of the organization a useful "snapshot" of the organization's "big picture."
- Give frontline employees a useful "touchstone" for their day-to-day decision making.
- Help individual employees understand the rationale behind organizational policy so they have confidence in resolving unique and unusual situations.
- Give customer contact employees and others insight into the things that are measured and monitored by your unit.

Here's what we've learned about the "power of purpose" to help create Knock Your Socks Off Service:

- If you do not have a definition of what good service means—your chances of getting high marks from your customers are about three in ten.
- If you have a very general definition—your chances of getting high marks from your customers improve to about fifty-fifty.
- If you have a detailed definition of what good service means—if it is defined in the context of both the *company* and the *customer*, if it is well communicated to employees, and tied to standards and measurement, your

chances of getting high marks from your customers are close to 90 percent.

Helping Employees Focus

A Statement of Service Focus isn't something simply to hang on the wall or pass out on laminated wallet cards. Once it exists, there are a multitude of ways to give it life and power.

• Test decisions against your service statement. Enlist one, two, perhaps even all of your employees to give you feedback on the consistency between your actions and the service strategy statement. And thank them for their help!

• Ask frontliners to use it to evaluate your unit's policies, procedures, and general "ways of doing things." Are they consistent with the service statement? Do they really help get things done for the customers? If not, where do they interfere with giving good service? And how can they be changed?

• Hold "what's stupid around here?" meetings. Use the focus statement to help identify outmoded practices, time-wasters, repeated trouble spots, and customer-vexing aspects of your business that make you look dumb, not smart, to your customers—and each other.

Set "stop, start, and measure" objectives. Perhaps once a quarter, ask every employee to come with a list of items under three headings:

1. Things we should stop doing around here.
2. Things we should start doing around here.
3. Things we don't track or measure—but should.

• Hold a "focus fantasy" meeting with your employees. Ask your people to discuss who they would like to be like: If they could model the business in general and their behaviors in particular after a famous or well-known organization, who would it be and why? McDonald's? American Express? Marriott? Milliken? Stew Leonard's Dairy? Federal Express? Or discuss what you would have to do differently to make the cover of the leading trade journal in your industry. Then act on what you hear.

The power of purpose is the power of knowing what to do, and when and how to do it, without having to be told. It helps your people take control of their work and their customers' experiences with your organization and frees them from the adolescent dependence on "management" that characterizes too many businesses today. It allows you to stop acting like a parent and start working with your people as adults.

If you take the service strategy as a lens through which to look from the inside out, you should see the things customers value and that can set your organization apart. If you use it as a lens to look from the outside in, you should get a consistent service focus that helps your people to work in "sync"—their actions in alignment with strategic goals.

> Setting and communicating the right expectations is the most important tool a manager has for imparting that elusive drive to the people he supervises.
>
> —Andrew S. Grove
> CEO, Intel Group

11

Getting Your Focus Down on Paper

The memory we want our guests to leave with is that of "I was treated special and cared about." So we look for lots of ways to "escort" our guests through every aspect of our hotel.

—Gary Jutz, General manager
Radisson Mark Plaza, Alexandria, Virginia

A good service strategy involves customers *and* employees. It takes on tangible shape and form when you actually put it on paper where everyone can see and use it. Don't overlook two important resources as you work to define your strategy:

• Customers are not only highly qualified, but generally willing to provide input that will help a company figure out what they want and don't want, how they do and don't want it delivered, and what elements of the service experience could be changed, improved, or removed for the business to serve them better.

• Employees are armed with an incredible amount of un-tapped information about customers and the types of service that leave a lasting, *positive* impression on them. And they know from firsthand experience where the weak spots and fail points are in even the most carefully devised service delivery system.

Words with Meaning

A service statement, service strategy, or customer pledge should be able to pass four quick tests:

1. It should be clear, concise, and understandable.
2. It should communicate, in actionable ways, the things you need to do to satisfy, impress, and keep your customers.
3. It should be consistent with other things you tell employees about the organization's mission and purpose.
4. It should pass the employee "snicker test": Reading it, whether on paper or out loud, should help your people better understand what to do, how to do it, and why to do it, not make them giggle, guffaw, and roll their eyes heavenward.

▲ *Remember:* Knock Your Socks Off Service is mostly a person-to-person activity. If your statement of service focus doesn't make it crystal clear how you want customers to feel (happy, entertained, secure, cared about, like they're dealing with professionals), it isn't complete.

No Put-On at the Ritz

When you see it done well, you just know it makes sense and helps in everything from measurement to motivation. Consider, for example, Ritz-Carlton Hotels. According to Ritz spokesperson Gayle MacIntyre, the company's service vision was put into words before the first property opened in 1983. As she explains it, Horst Schulze, president and COO, and his senior managers "believed that employees couldn't be expected to deliver first-rate, five-star service if management couldn't define it."

A good part of what Schulze and his management team came up with is embodied in the sixty-three-word statement of the Ritz-Carlton Credo and the twenty "Ritz-Carlton Basics" that define Knock Your Socks Off Service at the Ritz (see Figure 11-1).

Transforming Words to Action

Three steps are integral to service strategy formulation:

• Identify your key customers. For Radisson Hotel Corporation, it's the business traveler, a group comprising 80 percent of a business hotel's business. That doesn't mean Radisson doesn't jump to serve other customer groups. It just means the Radisson's service strategy, its systems, and its people are managed in a coordinated effort that is designed to segment and service that principal target market group.

• Identify your core contribution to customers. For airlines, it's moving things from point A to point B, on time, safely, with luggage intact and ideally on the same plane as the passenger who brought it to the airport. For a printing company, it's meeting the customer's need for high-quality documents that are produced on time and within budgets. In essence, your core contributions are the things you absolutely have to do to be in the business you're in.

• Decide what you want to be famous for. A service strategy ought to have some "jump start" component that makes you distinctive and exciting in the eyes of customers. Typically this is where there can be a clear and distinguishable difference between you and your competition. If your customers are going to be out there telling stories about you (the fabled "word of mouth" advertising that time and time again proves to be the most persuasive marketing edge you can have), this is what they're going to be talking about.

Once you've formulated your service strategy, you must communicate it over and over again. Just as 20:20 vision doesn't help the person who won't watch where he or she is going,

Figure 11-1.   Ritz-Carlton Credo and Basics.

*"We Are
Ladies and
Gentlemen
Serving
Ladies and
Gentlemen"*

THE RITZ-CARLTON

CREDO
●

The Ritz-Carlton Hotel is a place
where the genuine care and comfort
of our guests is our highest mission.

We pledge to provide the finest
personal service and facilities for our
guests who will always enjoy a warm,
relaxed yet refined ambience.

The Ritz-Carlton experience
enlivens the senses, instills well-
being, and fulfills even the
unexpressed wishes and needs
of our guests.

THREE STEPS
OF SERVICE

1
A warm and sincere greeting.
Use the guest name, if and
when possible.

2
Anticipation and compliance
with guest needs.

3
Fond farewell. Give them
a warm good-bye and use
their names, if and
when possible.

THE RITZ-CARLTON BASICS

1 The Credo will be known, owned and energized by all employees.
2 We are "Ladies and Gentlemen serving Ladies and Gentlemen".
3 The three steps of service shall be practiced by all employees.
4 "Smile" - "We are on stage". Always maintain positive eye contact.
5 Use the proper vocabulary with our guests. (Eliminate - Hello - Hi - OK - folks).
6 Uncompromising levels of cleanliness are the responsibility of every employee.
7 Create a positive work environment. Practice teamwork and "lateral service".
8 Be an ambassador of your hotel in and outside of the work place. Always talk positively - No negative comments.

9 Any employee who receives a guest complaint "owns" the complaint.
10 Instant guest pacification will be ensured by all. Respond to guest wishes within ten minutes of the request. Follow up with a telephone call within twenty minutes to ensure their satisfaction.
11 Use guest incident action forms to communicate guest problems to fellow employees and managers. This will help ensure that our guests are never forgotten.
12 Escort guests, rather than pointing out directions to another area of the hotel.
13 Be knowledgeable of hotel information (hours of operation, etc.) to answer guest inquiries.
14 Use proper telephone etiquette. Answer within three rings and, with a "smile", ask permission to put a caller on hold. Do not

screen calls. Eliminate call transfers when possible.
15 Always recommend the hotel's food and beverage outlets prior to outside facilities.
16 Uniforms are to be immaculate; Wear proper footwear (clean and polished) and your correct nametag.
17 Ensure all employees know their roles during emergency situations and are aware of procedures. (Practice fire and safety procedures monthly.)
18 Notify your supervisor immediately of hazards, injuries, equipment or assistance needs you have.
19 Practice energy conservation and proper maintenance and repair of hotel property and equipment.
20 Protecting the assets of a Ritz-Carlton Hotel is the responsibility of every employee.

your service strategy will mean nothing unless you and your employees can articulate and act on it.

I wish every employee could read our mission statement and know how it came about.

—Comment from a frustrated bank teller, penciled on a service quality survey

12

A Service Strategy
Statement Sampler

Write the vision, and make it plain upon tablets, that all
may readeth it.

—Habakkuk
Old Testament prophet

To help you craft your own service strategy statement, we offer
several examples. Notice that they come in all lengths, styles,
shapes, and sizes. Yours may resemble several, one, or none of
them. What matters is that your statement fits your company
and your customers.

Short and Sweet

If brevity is the soul of wit, it's worth measuring the words you
use carefully, making them count, not mount up. Here's how
a theme park and a restaurant chain "cut to chase":

CountryFair

The purpose of a theme park is to provide a setting
where people can have a large measure of good old-
fashioned fun. If people have fun in the park, they
will become both repeat customers and word-of-
mouth advocates of it. This theme park will work

74

when guests experience a *clean* entertainment environment, staffed by *friendly* people who provide good *service*, and find enjoyable *show* (games, rides, entertainments, food, and more) that the park and park people make available to them. When all that happens, the guests will say they are having a fun experience.

Country Kitchen

We make a very simple promise to all our guests: that our Country Kitchen is a warm, friendly place where they'll always feel welcome, just like in your mom's kitchen. (They can) come in any time of the day for meals cooked the way they like them . . . made from only the finest ingredients . . . and always served with a smile. Good country-cooked food . . . satisfying helpings . . . and fair prices.

Sometimes, articulating the whats, whys, and wherefores of your service strategy seems almost painfully simple—after you've completed the often arduous process of crafting it. As short and simple as the two statements above are, they've been abbreviated even further by employees:

- At CountryFair, they know the importance of "clean, friendly, service and show."
- At Country Kitchen, their goal is to make you "feel at home."

For Public and Private Consumption

A bit more in-depth are the following two examples. Both are intended to communicate with employees *and* with customers. Target, a national discount department store retailer, posts its service strategy statement right in the stores. Host International also is not shy about sharing its mission, vision, and values with customers in all of its stores (see Figure 12-1).

Figure 12-1. Host International's mission, vision, and values statement as it appears in its stores.

MISSION

We provide quality food, beverage and merchandise concessions in the travel and leisure industry; and we are focused on continually improving customer, landlord and associate satisfaction, and creating excellent long-term value for our shareholders.

VISION

WE WILL BE OUR CUSTOMERS' FIRST CHOICE.

VALUES

INTEGRITY

Treat associates, business partners and customers in an open, fair, honest and ethical manner.

CUSTOMER DRIVEN

Consistently meet or exceed all customers' expectations through a well-trained, motivated and equipped workforce that listens to customers and anticipates their changing needs.

PARTNERSHIP

Build mutually beneficial, sustaining relationships with landlords, airlines, business partners and local communities.

ECONOMIC VALUE

Increase shareholder value by making the best use of our capital and human resources.

TEAMWORK

Combine the energy and creativity of business partners and empowered associates, encouraging them to work to achieve the best solutions and performance for our business.

ASSOCIATES DEVELOPMENT

Offer all associates the opportunity and training to grow to their full potential while maintaining a balance between work and personal needs. Foster this growth in an environment that encourages open communication among all associates and that all find personally enriching, participatory and fun.

DIVERSITY

Create an environment that both values differences among associates, customers and business partners and removes any barriers to promoting women and minorities to all levels of management.

CREATIVITY

Develop an environment that rewards and encourages creativity and risk taking so that new and better ways of running the business are presented and tested on an ongoing basis.

Target Stores

This is our commitment to quality customer service.

No-hassle merchandise returns.

If you are unhappy with something you buy at Target, please return it for a quick, courteous exchange, adjustment, or refund. You can buy with confidence at Target.

Fast, accurate checkout.

We want checking out to be as pleasant and convenient as shopping. That means well-trained and friendly cashiers, scanning, correct and available price information, and quick service.

Assistance when you need it.

Self-service keeps Target prices low, yet when you need assistance you can depend on a quick, helpful response. Just ask any employee or pick up a red Customer Assistance Phone.

Merchandise you want when you want it.

You should expect us to be in stock on frequently purchased items and advertised merchandise. If we make a mistake and aren't, we will do whatever it takes to satisfy you without further inconvenience, including an immediate substitute or dependable raincheck for advertised merchandise.

Our commitment to you goes on and on.

We insist on sparkling clean stores. Clean restrooms. Quick check and credit approval. Shopper friendly store layout. Helpful product information. Carry-out service at your request. Friendly employees. And so much more!

If God Is in the Details . . .

For American Bankers Insurance Group, defining "The American Banker's Way" takes a lot of paper (see Figure 12-2). But it also provides important and actionable specifics, details that drive the efforts of each and every American Bankers employee and keeps the company focused with the power of purpose.

Where there is no vision, the people perish.

—Ecclesiastes

Figure 12-2. American Bankers' service strategy.

What makes American Bankers different from any other organization?

It's the Mission, Stategy, and Culture that have evolved and grown over the years. Some of this has happened by chance, and some of it has required careful planning and nurturing. By expressing all parts in written form, we now have a complete standard upon which each individual employee can base his business actions.

The American Bankers Ten Commandments reflect the culture of the company and are the informal guiding principles. They are a common sense view of how we conduct business. Each command-ment should be studied and constantly kept in mind.

The Boss's Bill of Rights is an important component of our corporate profile. The Bill of Rights, combined with the Mission, Strategy, and Ten Commandments, should lead you during your corporate life.

Our Corporate Mission states our reason for being in business.

The Corporate Strategy is management's guide for fulfilling the Corporate Mission.

Corporate Mission

To Sell, Through Affiliated Organizations, Innovative and Quality

(A) Insurance Products,

(B) Marketing, and

(C) Service

To Satisfy the Wants and Needs of the Middle Class Market.

Corporate Strategy

Marketing:

To establish profitable insurance under-writing, and service business in areas that are comparatively free of competi-tion, where we can excel in marketing.

To segment the marketplace by type of organization and distribution network, and form strategic business units to attack those market segments.

To achieve and maintain a dominant position in each market segment, an 8% return on sales and a compounded growth rate of 15%.

To market non-traditional insurance products through non-traditional distri-bution networks, acting as a manufac-turer and wholesaler of insurance products.

To establish a well compensated, trained, loyal sales force, selling by uniform methods in each of our market seg-ments.

To develop our businesses as appropriate in Canada, Europe and the Caribbean.

Administration

To provide the staff support and service needed by our sales force consistent with our Customer Service strategy and within the expense allowance provided by our premium rates.

To employ technology to automate administrative efforts for both the customer and ABIG.

To improve productivity through systems innovation, Streamline, value analysis and measured individual contributions.

To create continuity of management, opportunity for growth and personal sense of accomplishment for our personnel.

To create a working environment where all employees are aware that they are each an integral part of the sales effort.

To employ and develop loyal, highly motivated and well trained employees.

Financial

To provide the shareholders consistent annual growth and earnings per share and a return on equity above alternative investments with similar risks.

To maximize investment return, giving due regard to ultimate safety of principal

with investment results in the upper industry quartile.

To maintain a favorable balance of debt to equity and other key financial ratios.

To employ control disciplines which monitor profit experience and take appropriate action.

To periodically evaluate all business segments against the corporate cost of capital and provide adequate capital as required by each affiliate.

Service

To serve The Boss (our customer) with integrity and responsible care, following the "Boss's Bill of Rights." Above all, resolve the Boss's problems quickly.

American Bankers' Ten Commandments

I. You never get in trouble for what you do, only for doing nothing. (It is right to say, "I was wrong.")

II. Stay out of the mainstream of competition and excel in product innovation and marketing.

III. To make a profit you must follow the A,B,C's—Adequate premium, Better claims handling, Common sense underwriting. (There are 100 cents in a dollar. Learn to add to 100.)

IV. The most important person in the Company is the one who makes the sale. (Our agents and accounts are critical to our business. They will be treated respectfully and with dignity.)

V. Executive management has the prerogative and responsibility to question anyone and everything. (So does everyone else.)

VI. When you take over a piece of business ask, "Why are we so lucky?"

VII. You don't get authority, you get accountability.

VIII. To be a low cost quality operation you must have productive, well trained, motivated people.

IX. The most important personal qualities are integrity and persistence.

X. Never back anyone into a corner.

Customer Service Strategy

At American Bankers, Service Is The Difference!

We Care About Our Customers And Commit Ourselves To Quality Customer Service By:

Providing innovative and competitive products designed to meet the needs and expectations of our customers.

Delivering quick response by knowledgeable and highly motivated employees who believe the customer is Boss.

Striving for reliable and consistent

support delivered by accounting, claims and processing areas.

We Insure This Commitment By:

Actively soliciting the needs and opinions of our customers.

Continuously reviewing our company policies and procedures for customer ease of access.

Providing training, award opportunities and measurable service standards for each of our employees.

The Boss's Bill of Rights

Who is the most important person to you? The Boss! At American Bankers the Boss is our accounts and customers. Without them your livelihood and our Company would cease to exist. The Boss's rights must be protected. These are the guidelines.

1. Meet the Boss's expectations as well as his needs.

2. Make solving the Boss's problems your first priority.

3. Hire, train, motivate, and reward employees who are:

   Caring   Competent
   Professional   Enthusiastic

4. Set up monitor procedures to ensure that the Boss's call and correspondence go to the right place . . . the first time.

5. Communicate with the Boss in a non-technical manner avoiding difficult insurance terms and concepts.

6. Always answer the Boss's call within three rings.

7. Always return the Boss's call within 24 hours.

8. Always respond to the Boss's letter within 5 days.

9. Ensure timely and fair payment of the Boss's claims.

10. Remember "The most important person in the company is the one who makes the sale." And, in every communication, you continue to make the sale!

A Vision of American Bankers in the '90s

American Bankers has become a leader by constantly working to improve every aspect of our business. As we approach the 1990s and the 21st Century, we will strive to create:

■ The country's finest distributing insurance company with more and better channels of distribution

■ Unique and innovative products for every business segment

■ Competitive advantage through the use of technology

■ Highly productive, motivated, disciplined personnel—achieving, and being properly rewarded

■ An organization where the customer is boss; where we have a relationship that generates respect, and our service is perceived as best

■ An excellent A, B, C* Profit Control System

■ A flexible, useful management accounting system.

The creation of these values will result in the forging of a strong and growing company which will be a leader in profitability, market share, and increase in shareholder value.

* A — Adequate Premium

  B — Better Claims Handling

  C — Common Sense Underwriting

Imperative 4

Make Your Service Delivery System ETDBW (Easy to Do Business With)

Your service delivery system is all of the apparatus, physical and procedural, that the employees of your organization must have at their disposal to meet customers' needs and to keep the service promises you make to your customers. A well designed service delivery system will make you easy to do business with. What your service strategy promises is what your system must deliver. Every time.

If your promise is, "twenty-four-hour delivery on all orders—no exceptions," your service delivery system is everything you do and use to make twenty-four-hour delivery a reality, from your order entry system to the way you measure your performance.

In a badly designed and poorly operating delivery system, you frequently hear *managers* complaining about lazy, unmotivated employees, *frontline employees* complaining about stupid, unreasonable customers, and *customers* complaining about inflexible, unhelpful people and rules. A well-done service delivery system is customer- and employee-friendly and has monitors and feedback mechanisms to enable the people who work in the system to correct poor results.

Your continuing quest should be to seek out ways of making it easier for your customers to do business with you tomorrow than it was for them to do business with you last year, last month, last week, and last night.

Rest assured, that's exactly what your competition is doing.

Never say, "That's against company policy," unless you have a good explanation to back up the policy.

—Mary Kay Ash
Founder, Mary Kay Cosmetics

13

Bad Systems Stop Good People

You can take great people, highly trained and motivated, and put them in a lousy system and the system will win every time.

—Geary Rummler
President, The Rummler-Bache Group

Kathy Ridge, president of Ridge Consulting & Training, Charlotte, North Carolina, tells the story of going to the grocery store one evening to buy food for the family of a friend who was spending a few days in the hospital. When she asked about getting a deli tray, she was informed by the night clerk that the woman who made them up had already left for the evening. "I didn't know making deli trays was such a specialized skill," was Kathy's first response. But meats and cheeses still seemed like a good idea, so she decided to create her own deli assortment piece by piece.

She asked the clerk to thin-slice a half pound of ham. He did, wrapping the slices in waxed butcher paper, writing the price on the package and putting it on the deli counter. The process was repeated with turkey, then roast beef, then Swiss cheese, then . . . About the time Kathy had more than $20 worth of food on the counter, she noticed a stack of large empty plastic deli trays on a back table. Sudden inspiration: "How much for one of those with a plastic lid?"

"Lady," came the tart response, "you can't buy a tray unless you buy a *tray*."

"Excuse me?"

"YOU CAN'T BUY A TRAY UNLESS YOU BUY A *TRAY*."

Kathy's first surmise was that she was dealing with a frontline person in desperate need of a personality transplant. Belatedly, she realized the real issue: the store's inventory control *system* was based on counting the trays. It wasn't that the clerk didn't want to help her. He just couldn't see how to.

The system won. The customer lost. The frontline person lost, too. The people who decided to use deli trays as a financial control device no doubt had the best of intentions. But they were blind to the effects of their decision on customers. And the organization's obviously well communicated insistence on following procedures to the letter stopped the frontline service person in his tracks. The net result? Kathy Ridge was moved to discover a better store in which to buy not only deli trays, but all of her groceries.

Yes, you need systems. But rules, policies, and procedures should be servants, not masters. In a world where most services are readily available from multiple sources, it is important to make the system component of the service transaction at a minimum painless and easy, at best invisible or positively memorable.

Your frontline people have nothing but the system and their own skills to use in satisfying customers. A well-designed service system must have two attributes if it is to help them do that consistently:

1. *Service delivery systems should be "easy on the front line."* Service delivery systems are not a naturally occurring phenomenon in nature. People make them up. People should be able to explain them, and adjust them, and fine-tune them, and change them—and even circumvent them on those occasions when a customer comes in from an angle no system designer could ever have foreseen. The people with the power to flex the systems should be the ones at the front line.

2. *Service delivery systems should be "easy for the front line."* If the rules, policies, and procedures get in the way of giving

great service, your people will in time stop focusing on their roles and start focusing on their restrictions. As one veteran of the frontline wars told us, "If I'm on the front line and customers bitch about barriers I can't better or bypass, I'll either become a bastard or burn out."

The Human Factor

There's a very real people dimension to the system dilemma. It's usually expressed in the lament, "You just can't get good people anymore." Wrong. We would argue that generations of experience with dysfunctional and sometimes downright abusive service systems have taught our frontline people—and our customers—a lot of bad habits, attitudes, and behaviors. The people at the front line have learned to duck and cover because what hits the fan hits them from every direction.

For years, higher-ups have preached conformity to rules and regulations, policies and procedures, accountability and control—and made a point of punishing people who got a little uppity and tried to do more than they were allowed to do. As a result, customers faced with inflexible people and their inflexible rules learned to get nasty if they wanted to receive anything beyond the letter of the policy manual. It's truly a vicious circle.

If you think you have bad service people, fix the system to make it livable and responsive for everyone involved. You'll be amazed by the human changes you'll create.

The Law of Rules

Your task as a manager is to set up workflows, guidelines, procedures, and fail-safes that your people can readily manipulate to meet the specific needs and expectations of your customers. It's inevitable that rules will be written or evolve over time. The "good rules" will serve your people—and through them your customers—well. The "bad rules" will seek to enslave. How do you know which is what?

- *Good rules* are grounded in customer expectations and contribute to meeting customer needs. Making answering the phone by the third ring into a rule won't help the customer whose call is answered in staccato fashion and put on hold before a word can be inserted edgewise because your people are working only to hit the statistical target.
- *Good rules* help the customer experience the service provider as "easy to do business with." Put yourself in your customer's shoes: Do the steps you're asked to take make sense or make extra work for you?
- *Good rules* are consistent with your service strategy. Kinko's Copy Centers work hard to be the copier of choice for college students. Consequently, the Kinko's rule of thumb is "We accept students' checks."
- *Good rules* are consistent with the partnership (co-creator) dimension of service. If your customers are truly your partners, then the pieces and parts of your service system have to provide mutual benefits. They need to help you serve; they need to help your customers/partners tell you how you can serve them better.
- *Good rules* have feedback woven in. They have a system monitoring component that alerts your people in prompt and actionable fashion whenever the delivery system is about to fail or break. That way you can fix it before your customer experiences the disappointment of service breakdown.
- *Good rules* allow your frontline people to be human, not robots. They allow—even encourage—your people to respond uniquely, personally, and creatively to the full spectrum of customer needs and expectations . . . and especially to those that do not fit the standard pattern.
- *Good rules* remind everyone that they are guidelines to promote a value or goal, *not* the value or goal itself. Like our rule-restricted deli clerk, if your people follow the letter of the law but miss the value or goal, they've failed themselves, the organization, and most especially the customer.

When applied without customer focus to a service delivery system, the legacy of production (with its focus on control, uniformity, measurability, accountability, scientific method, and linear thinking) leads to noncreative, nonresponsive people and actions. It causes service people to "step over dollars to pick up dimes." And all in full view of the customer—who's expecting better of you.

In setting up, fail-safing, and continuously evaluating your service system, remember that it's the *customer's* need that is driving the game. As Harvard marketing professor Theodore Levitt puts it, the customer would like to go from "I need a quarter-inch hole" to "I have a quarter-inch hole" without having to deal with quarter-inch drill bits and drills and hardware stores and chucks and electric cords and checkout counters. The smart service provider designs and maintains the delivery system accordingly.

> Service systems that are low on the friendliness scale tend, by their very design, to subordinate convenience and ease of access for the customer in favor of the convenience of the people within the system.
>
> —Karl Albrecht
> Co-author, Service America

14

Fix the System, Not the People

Eighty percent of customers' problems are caused by bad systems, not by bad people.

—John Goodman
President, TARP, Inc.

Your people can only be as good as your system allows them to be. So ask yourself how much of the complexity you can take out of your system. The simpler, faster, easier, and user-friendlier you can make it for your customers, and your employees, the more willing and skilled they'll become at making use of it.

Warning Signs

Any time you hear a sales or service person—or yes, even a manager—say things like the following to a customer, you are listening to a service delivery system that is not easy to do business with:

"I'm sorry, it's against policy."
"Well, just wait a couple more days. I'm sure it'll show up soon."
Customer: "Can I ask you a question?" Service Rep: "Make it quick, I've got a meeting to go to."

"Ma'am, we wouldn't have given your name to a collection agency if you hadn't been billed at *least* twice."

"Oh, that's a sales floor (or warehouse, or accounting, or field service) problem. I'm in customer service. No, I don't have that number."

"My computer is down, can you call back later?"

"I know you're not ready to leave yet, but would you mind paying your bill? I'm going off duty in fifteen minutes."

And the all-time champion chant of the dysfunctional service system:

"You have to understand how we do business here."

System Solutions

The operative theme is being "easy to do business with" (ETDBW)—how's that for a mystifying acronym to toss into your next memo or managerial pronouncement? It is a, if not *the*, critical customer imperative for the 1990s.

How good are you right now? How many times do you have to wonder "Where did the system break down" and "Where did the customer get lost" and "How can we rewrite the rules, change the policies, or upgrade the gear to keep this from happening again?" The more you ask (and answer) those questions in the short term, the less you'll face them as problems in the long term.

Here's a little ETDBW experiment to find out where you are right now.

ETDBW Quick Test

1. Go out for lunch or coffee, or do something to get you out of the building.
2. Call home—back to your office/department/store, using the general, in-the-phonebook number, not the one you know to call when you want fast action.
3. Without identifying yourself (disguise your voice if you

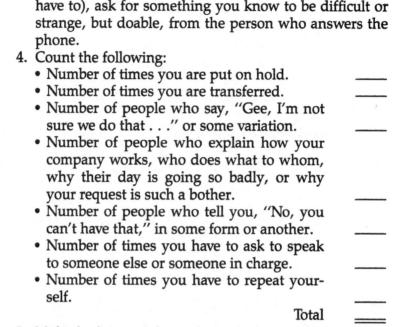

have to), ask for something you know to be difficult or strange, but doable, from the person who answers the phone.

4. Count the following:
   - Number of times you are put on hold. ____
   - Number of times you are transferred. ____
   - Number of people who say, "Gee, I'm not sure we do that . . ." or some variation. ____
   - Number of people who explain how your company works, who does what to whom, why their day is going so badly, or why your request is such a bother. ____
   - Number of people who tell you, "No, you can't have that," in some form or another. ____
   - Number of times you have to ask to speak to someone else or someone in charge. ____
   - Number of times you have to repeat yourself. ____

                                           Total ____

5. Multiply the result by 10 and subtract from 150 to arrive at your "Easy To Do Business With" quotient. Your ETDBW quotient is like an IQ: The lower it is, the harder you are to do business with.

ETDBW Scores

125–150:   Genius—Your systems are an asset.

100–124:   Average—Your systems aren't any worse than anybody else's.

75–99:   Slow—Your systems are a detriment to customer retention.

below 75:   Disabled—Your systems are probably driving customers away in droves. Immediate remedial action indicated.

Improving Your ETDBW IQ

What does an Easy To Do Business With service delivery system look like in action? From the customer's point of view, the "customer friendliest" delivery systems are:

1. *Accessible.* You can reach the company easily and when you want to.
2. *Accurate.* Whether it's about shipments, billings, or status, the information is accurate and correct.
3. *Integrated.* Customers can get all the information they need from one point of contact.
4. *Customer-driven.* Customers can understand and use the information they're given without a basket of order and item and billing code numbers at hand.
5. *Fast.* Customers never have the sense they are waiting for a very slow computer to get warmed up or that their order is making the trip from Phoenix to Boston via rickshaw or pedicab.
6. *Totally transparent.* If there are hoops to be jumped through or marathons to be run, they happen outside of the customer's field of vision.

Changing a "Not so ETDBW" System

- *Do not* go out and start buying new computers or a new phone system.
- *Do not* go out and hire a pack of expensive management consultants.
- *Do not* blame, punish, or execute your frontline people.
- *Do* start with a series of small meetings with customer contact employees and employees who directly support their work. (Don't make the meetings too small or people will be reluctant to tell you what they really think or so large that most people feel like spectators.) In those meetings ask two questions:

1. What do our customers like least about doing business with us?
2. What can we do to make it easier for you to serve the customer?

Then shut up, listen, and take notes. You won't necessarily like the answers, and they may not all be immediately actionable, but they will give you a great start at making your company, department, or team Easy To Do Business With.

> We believe that our activities should be governed by the needs and desires of our customers rather than by our internal requirement and insights.
>
> —Eugene F. McCabe
> Vice president, Marketing,
> Merck Sharpe & Dohme

15

Measure and Manage From the Customer's Point of View

The four most important words in service quality are:
measure, measure, measure, and measure.

—Ken Dagley
President,
Australian Customer Service Association

Regardless of the business you are in and the size of your operation, measure you must! A commitment to service quality without a commitment to standards and measurement is a dedication to lip service, not customer service. Standards and measurement are critical to the smooth functioning—and improvement—of your service delivery system.

A common denominator among companies with reputations for high quality service is their bias for setting service standards and their prodigious efforts to measure how well those standards are met. In complex service delivery systems—like those of United Parcel Service, MCI, and Southwest Airlines—that effort involves hundreds of standards and a multitude of measurement systems to keep service delivery on an even keel. In a simpler system, like that of a McGuffey's

Restaurant or the Insty-Prints or Kinko's down on the corner, it takes far fewer standards and measures to keep on top of the "How are we doing?" question.

The Look of Customer-Focused Measurement

Chances are pretty good that your company already measures a number of things about the service delivery systems you manage all or part of. Just the same, it is a good idea to stop, step back from your system for a moment, and ask yourself whether your current measurement is driven by customer parameters or internal technical specs. To make sure the former, not the latter, energizes your measurement efforts, use these three general criteria for auditing—and perhaps improving—the customer focus of your service delivery system.

1. Your measurements should reflect your "purpose." Nothing makes your vision or service strategy—your purpose—more real to your frontline employees than measuring what you're doing against customer-focused norms.

If your service promise is for "timely deliveries on all shipments" and your customers have told you that means "twenty-four-hour turnaround on all orders," measure that. But don't just look inside. You're not done until the customer has taken delivery, so be sure you also measure the customer's perception of whether or not orders are arriving "in a timely fashion." Even if you're dead solid certain that a customer's order came and went in twenty-four hours—and twenty-four hours is twice as good as your nearest competitor—if the customer doesn't "feel" that the order arrived in a timely fashion, the customer is right and you are wrong.

▲ *Remember:* For the customer, *perception* is all there is!

How can you be 100 percent "on time" but wrong about being "timely"?

- First, the twenty-four hour standard is *your* technical standard, not the customer's. To the customer, "timely" is a perception, not a measurement, as it is to you.
- Second, "timely" or "on-time" to you typically means when the order goes out *your* door. To customers, those same words may well mean the time the order comes in *their* door, is on the shelf in *their* warehouse, or is in hand and ready for distribution or use in *their* system.

Not your problem? Wrong! If your customers believe there is a problem, there is a problem—whether you think it's real or not. And you'd better have a systematic way of finding out about it. Your measurement system has to tell you about the problems customers are perceiving, and as soon as possible, not just comfort you with statistics about your adherence to your own technical standards.

2. Your measurements should measure customer quality, not just technical quality. There is a difference between the two.

- *Technical quality* is the measurement of all the mechanical and procedural things that must go right if your system is to work effectively and efficiently. Technical quality measures are *internal* indicators of your delivery system's specification driven performance.

▲ *Think:* Down time, order waiting time, order assembly time, back order volume, order turnaround time, shipments per hour, time per phone call, and similar measures.

- *Customer quality* is the performance of your service delivery system from the *customer's* point of view. It is the assembly of elements that are important to the customer, as judged by the customer. These are the elements that are directly observable by the customer and that most directly determine their satisfaction with your service delivery system.

▲ *Think:* Ease of contact, order correctness and completeness, timeliness of order arrival, courtesy of people dealt with, look of package upon arrival, understandability of the bill, and similar subjective impressions.

Technical quality measures are important to trouble spotting, problem solving, and the smooth and cost-effective functioning of the system. Customer quality measures are important to customer satisfaction and retention, and to system improvement and priority setting.

3. Your measurements should measure what's important, not just what's handy. It's late at night. A man, call him Naz, is crawling about on hands and knees in the street, near a streetlight. Chaz, a neighbor, comes by, watches Naz feeling around, sifting through the dirt, and crawling about.

"What are you looking for, old friend?" he asks.

"My key," answers Naz. "I lost my door key and can't get in my house."

"Just exactly where were you when you last saw your key?"

"Oh," answers Naz as he continues his searching, "I was across the street, near my front door when I dropped it."

"Then why are you looking for your key way over here?"

"Because the light's better over here," answers Naz.

That story must be over 400 years old and a staple at scout skit-nights. But, like Naz, we're all prone from time to time to do things the easy way, not the best way. That's especially true of building service quality measures.

In organizations with extensive telephone customer contact, for example, the two most common measurements of the delivery system are length of phone calls and number of rings before pick-up. Yet customers we've asked about contact with such companies seldom if ever mention either factor. They're more concerned about getting the information they need, having their problems solved (ideally during that first contact), and not being put on hold for hours or connected to the voicemail system from hell.

In some companies, these two measures have been automated and computerized as an employee surveillance and evaluation system. The claim is that such measurement systems improve service. They do not. They *may* improve productivity, which may or may not be related, but service is *not* the point of such measurement systems. Authority and accountability are.

Not only do they not have the desired effect on customers, they also don't do a thing to help the people charged with delivering customer service. We've yet to talk to a frontline service worker hooked up to one of these electronic stopwatch systems who didn't: (1) resent the obvious lack of trust and (2) learn to trick the system anyway in self-defense. (How? Easy: Watch the time and hang up in mid-sentence when the call starts to go too long. If and when the mystified—or disgruntled—customer calls back, apologize . . . and blame it on "equipment failure.")

Are we suggesting that you not measure "number of rings before answer" or "length of talk-time with customer"? No. We are saying that these and similar measurements, valuable as they may or may not be for managing costs and monitoring system capacity, are not necessarily helping you directly manage service quality as perceived by your customer. And that means they're not helping—and may well be hindering—your people as they try to directly improve customer satisfaction and directly build customer retention.

Effective service delivery measurements are not only customer-focused, they are extensive and comprehensive. They measure a lot of things, and they do it in a lot of ways. The following checklist should give you some ideas and encourage you to spread your measurement net wider.

A Checklist for Measuring

1. Are you gathering information from every useful source?
   - customers
   - distributors
   - suppliers
   - dealers
   - employees

2. Are you measuring frequently enough? Does your "measurement cycle" match your "service cycle"?
3. Are your questions fair? Do they tap technical specifications, customer experiences, and customer perceptions?
4. Are all measurements displayed where employees can see the results? Are results displayed in simple, straightforward averages and ratios that are easy for all to understand?
5. Do you benchmark your delivery system against competitors? Against the most respected service provider in your geographical area? Against "best of the best" companies, regardless of industry or geography?
6. Are the data you collect and display useful? Can they be used to improve technical systems? Can individuals as well as teams use them to improve performance?
7. Is your measurement qualitative (opinions and impressions) as well as quantitative (numbers)? Are both displayed and discussed in your department? Quickly—while the information is still fresh enough to be used with confidence and effect?
8. Is there an easily understandable connection between measurement results and organizational consequences? Between results and personal consequences? Since "what gets rewarded gets repeated," are you really measuring what you want repeated?

As a supervisor or firstline manager, you may not have a lot of control over what gets measured and how it gets measured. But by thinking through what your current measurement does and does not give you, and how you are and are not using the results, you can affect the performance of your delivery system. And if you're not getting the kind of data you need—or getting too much of the wrong kind of data—it's in your interest to build a case with the keepers of the measurement flame for changing this unproductive state of affairs. And the sooner the better!

'Tain't nowhere near right, but it's approximately correct.

> —Howland Owl (Pogo's Quality Guru,
> explaining the inbred weaknesses of all
> measurement systems)

16

Add Value: The Milk and Cookies Principle

He who gives great service gets great returns.

—Elbert Hubbard
19th-century American writer

Great systems, well-designed and managed, start with a simple goal: reliability—delivering on your *core promise* to the customer. An airline that promises to take you from New York to Minneapolis, but deposits you in Indianapolis instead, does not make you a happy traveler, no matter how great the onboard food, or how nice the cabin crew, or how smooth the ride.

But that's just for starters. How do you compete for customers when you are one of three airlines, each boasting five flights a day between New York and Minneapolis, all of which deliver passengers to the right "apolis" safely, on time and with most of their luggage in hand?

Taking off and landing uneventfully will make you just one of three carriers that meet the basic core requirement of "airline" on the LGA-MSP route. To distinguish yourself, your systems will need to help you reliably and consistently offer something "extra," an added value, to distinguish your style of doing business and attract business away from your competitors.

Preplanned Value-Added

The frequent-customer programs developed as value-addeds by airlines, hotels, car rental companies, and even department stores and grocery stores, are clearly preplanned. Our favorite example of the type of no-charge extras that can be bundled in, tracked, and consistently repeated to win over and keep customers is the Doubletree Inn's Milk and Cookies program. Frequent business travelers who stay with this Phoenix-based lodging company answer a number of personal preference questions the first time they sign in at a company property. Among the questions: "Would you like a complimentary plate of chocolate chip cookies and a glass of milk before bedtime when you stay with us?" If the answer is yes, Doubletree's computers remember that preference as long as those customers continue to have a bedtime sweet tooth. And each time they check in at another Doubletree, the system makes sure there are milk and cookies waiting for them.

Other common preplanned value-addeds include:

- Breaking shipments into customer-specified portions rather than giving them standard take-it-or-leave-it lot sizes.
- Timing shipments to arrive when the customer wants them to arrive, not simply when it's convenient for your carrier.
- Changing billing dates and forms to fit the customer's systems.
- Making product modifications to fit customer needs and peculiarities.
- Applying special discounts to long term preorders.

Spontaneous Value-Addeds

The other form of added value comes from flexing your systems periodically for the customer on a one-time, creative, "wouldn't it be nice if we . . ." basis. Frequently these are small but memorable gestures that customers recall as engaging "personal touches" but that reflect good system design. When appropriate and doable, these are among the most memorable value-addeds.

We have a friend who can't stop telling the story of a recent value-added experience with the Taj Mahal in Atlantic City. She was maid of honor at a wedding that turned into an impromptu excursion for dancing and gambling after the reception. As the first of the wedding party to arrive at the hotel, without reservations, she let the front desk staff know of the group that was on its way and left a message for the newlyweds to call her room once they'd checked in.

When the phone rang twenty minutes later, she found herself talking to an elated couple who unexpectedly found themselves in a luxurious suite, courtesy of the hotel. Instead of robotically processing another arrival, the service person on the night desk had taken the liberty—it being a slow night in the hotel—to add a little unexpected value to the experience. The Taj Mahal figures to be an annual anniversary destination for the newlyweds as well as the number one choice for the others when they go looking for a special night on a special town.

Eight Times to Do Value-Addeds

1. For the good, solid, steady, no-complaints, no-noise customer. Unspectacular, uncomplaining, salt-of-the-earth customers are often the most neglected. It's easy to take them for granted. It isn't easy to replace them with similarly good-natured people. If you do business with North Carolina-based Wilson Fence Company, expect to receive a letter beginning, "All too often, we do business with nice people, such as yourself, and then go on as if nothing had ever happened or without giving the customer a second thought. We would like to take a few minutes out of a busy day to personally thank you for your business."

2. For the customer who has done you the favor of complaining. By bringing a real or potential problem to your

attention, complaining customers are giving you a chance (1) to regain their loyalty and goodwill, and (2) spot and fix problem areas in your service system that other customers might suffer through in silence. Robert Jones, CEO of JP Hotels, which owns several Holiday Inn franchise properties in the eastern United States, sends a personal "Thank you for bringing it to my attention" note to any customer who complains via comment card, letter, or phone call.

3. For a new customer who has just placed a second order or increased the level of business they are doing with you. Our favorite American Speedy Printing Centers franchise in Minneapolis doesn't take new business as its due. New customers receive a special information packet, hand-delivered by the store manager, along with a gift jar (embossed with the Speedy address and phone number, of course!) filled with candy. Is yours empty? Let 'em know—they'll refill it when they deliver your next printing job.

4. For a customer who has thanked you. When someone goes out of their way to express their gratitude for something you've done in the course of your business relationship with them, you have a tremendous opportunity to deepen and strengthen the bond by responding in kind. A good friend wrote to Ralston-Purina to let the company know just how much her cat enjoyed Purina Cat Chow—Tabby wouldn't even touch other brands, would actually pick out the Purina pieces and leave the rest if her owner tried to mix two together. A few weeks after writing, the cat owner received a thank-you note. And a coupon. She was surprised, but she shouldn't have been.

5. For a customer who has been through a difficult time. When things don't go smoothly, but your customer hangs in there with you, or when a loyal customer has learned the true meaning of Murphy's Law, a little "something for nothing" and corporate TLC is clearly in order. A woman who regularly shopped Stew Leonard's Connecticut dairy store went home empty-handed one evening when the computerized cash registers crashed. She couldn't wait for the system to come back on line because that evening was her husband's birthday, a fact

she shared with a store manager when she called to offload a little frustration. In short order, a Stew Leonard's station wagon arrived with her groceries—and a cake with the frosted greeting "Happy Birthday from Stew and the Gang."

6. When going out of your way will prevent a customer from having a problem. Cleo Lloyd of White's Office Supply in Kannapolis, North Carolina, became our favorite store manager when he showed up on the doorstep one evening, twenty minutes before it was time to dash for the airport, with a box of blank transparency sheets we'd had on back order but had forgotten to pick up. He knew our business well enough to know we used such materials in presentations and had obviously been paying attention the day before when we talked about the need for the sheets on an approaching trip.

7. For a good customer who has the potential for bringing you new customers or increased business. Word-of-mouth advertising is more persuasive than any other kind. It's absolutely permissible to put words in the mouths of customers whose endorsement of your services can serve as a significant professional reference for your business. Adding a free car wash to a tune-up for Mr. Jones makes good sense for the local Flying Flivver dealership—especially if Mr. Jones is the purchasing manager for ABC Widgets and the person who buys ABC's company cars.

8. Anyone for whom you feel like doing a "good deed." Sometimes giving a little value-added service just makes you feel good, regardless of whether or not it directly affects future business. So like the Nike ads say, "Just Do It!" Don't overlook your internal customers—your people—in the value-added process. At McGuffey's Restaurants in Asheville, North Carolina, employees receive ABCD (Above and Beyond the Call of Duty) sweatshirts when they provide unexpected pluses to restaurant customers.

> We view "Going the Extra Mile" service as an honor—not an obligation.
>
> —Hal Stringer
> President, Peerless Systems, Inc.

17

Make Recovery a Point of Pride . . . and a Part of Your System

> There are two kinds of companies. The first, the most typical, views complaints as a disease to be got over, with memory of the pain rapidly suppressed. The second . . . views the complaint as a luscious opportunity.
>
> —Tom Peters and Nancy Austin
> *A Passion For Excellence*

All around the country, frontline service people are having to deal with customers who experience service failure. It's not their fault, anymore than it's the customers' (although it's worth pointing out that about 30 percent of all problems with products and services are indeed *caused* by customers).

No service system is or ever will be 100 percent perfect. Sooner or later, something will go wrong. When it does, how your front line responds not only can make the best of a bad situation, but it can actually turn disappointment into customer satisfaction—sometimes even into customer delight! Hence the term *recovery*.

Service recovery includes all the actions your people take to get a disappointed customer back to a state of satisfaction. Like the hospital staff or doctor nursing a sick patient back to health, service recovery is returning the customer "back to normal."

But great service recovery does not happen by luck, or solely through the interpersonal skills of your frontline people. Effective service recovery is planned and managed. It's a system that has to be designed and used just like any other system in your business. And your people have to know how to make it work on the customer's behalf.

Speak No Evil?

You may be asking yourself, "Is this service recovery stuff something we even need to talk about? Why not just put our energy into doing it right the first time? And, besides, maybe talking about mistakes will cause mistakes to happen more often—sort of a Pygmalion effect. Shouldn't our goal be zero defects? Shouldn't we accentuate the positive and eliminate the negative, as the old song used to advise?"

If service were always (or even mostly) perfect, we wouldn't need to talk about it. But it isn't. Service is neither designed nor delivered in a high-tech clean room, where no contaminants can get into the process. It happens on the sales floor, in drive-through lanes, over the phone, with the involvement of third parties, and subject to the disruptive influence of everything that is going on around it.

Recovery Defined

Instead of shuddering at the very mention of a potential problem, it's far better to prepare your people and the systems they work with to handle those occasional shortfalls. Keep in mind that customers have very different and unique requirements for "what is good service." A small mistake that causes one customer to say "ah, no problem" can make another customer livid.

Over the last several years, we've spent a lot of time researching the whys and wherefores of service recovery. Consistently, we find six caring actions that combine to make service recovery systematic, memorable, and satisfying.

1. Apologize. The point is not to determine who's to blame. It's to solve the problem. If your customers have a problem, chances are they're not happy. The first step to problem solving is to acknowledge the fact that—at least in the customers' eyes—a problem exists. So start by having your people tell them, personally and sincerely, "I'm sorry."

2. Listen and empathize. This is not the time to instruct customers in the finer points of what they should have done to avoid the problem in the first place. Customers resent being lectured to. What they mostly want your people to do right now is just listen. Listening and empathizing helps customers unwind, get it out of their systems, and feel they're talking to someone who really cares about taking care of things.

3. "Fair fix" the problem. After listening (so they know exactly what's at issue), your people can snap to and, based on customer information and suggestions, work to resolve the problem. Usually, what customers want now is what they wanted originally—and the sooner the better.

4. Offer atonement. Your recovery system will earn high marks from customers if it includes, even symbolically, some form of atonement that, in a manner appropriate to the issue at hand, says, "I'd like to make it up to you."

5. Keep your promises. Recovery time is double jeopardy "where the stakes are doubled and the scores can really change." Your system has already failed once. If your people make promises they can't keep in trying to get your business back in the customer's good graces, it will be gas on the fire. Employees need to know how to be realistic about what they can and can't deliver, and how quickly.

6. Follow up. In a few days, or a few weeks, have your people check back to make sure things really did work out to your customer's satisfaction. That kind of thoroughness and demonstrated concern builds loyalty that can weather future storms.

Implementing Recovery

Once you have a recovery system in place, you have to factor in three important modifiers that govern the process from the customer's standpoint.

1. Customers have expectations for how effective service recovery should happen. Of course, you cannot learn what the customer expects unless and until you ask, which means soliciting complaints. There's solid data on the value of that orientation. Remember that only one dissatisfied customer in twenty-five complains. Yet complaining customers can actually become more loyal than customers who pronounce themselves satisfied . . . if they've been listened to and responded to in a way that says you want them to come back again, despite this momentary glitch.

What does this mean to you as a manager? It means looking at customer feedback as a gift. When you get complaints from customers, share the information at the front line in a positive, not punitive, fashion. Rather than seek to find a guilty party, show your people that your objective is to retain the customer. If you shoot the messenger, your frontline people will neither encourage customer feedback nor report to you the service problems they identify. You'll never find your fail points until it's too late.

What's more, whenever you receive a complaint, you should see and hear not one whining malcontent but twenty-five valuable corporate assets assembled around your desk and deciding whether they ever want to come back and do business with you again.

2. When customers experience a service breakdown, they need to be fixed as well as their problems. Relationships are built on trust. A bad experience with you hacks away at that trust and creates an expectation (actually, a dread) that the same thing will happen the *next* time, too. That's why you want your people to listen and empathize first, then start asking problem-resolution questions.

Make sure they know how to respond to the Smokescreen Principle. Complaining customers often start by throwing up an emotional, sometimes even irrational, smokescreen first to find out how serious you are about listening to them. If your people dismiss the ranting and raving out of hand as sheer exaggeration, they're missing the point. Customers aren't used to having someone listen when they complain. This is their way of testing how serious you are. If you pass the test and get past that smokescreen, they will calm themselves down to the point that you get the rational, logical stuff, which is what you need to fix the problem. The emotional stuff is not going to help you fix the problem. But unless and until you get through it to the real issues, there's not much you can really accomplish.

3. Effective planning leads to effective service recovery. Top service providers identify places in their delivery system where service predictably fails and customers are left disappointed. They then outline service recovery standards to provide frontline people guidance in how to handle the customer who has been victimized. Although every situation is somewhat unique, guidance and clarity of expectations can provide frontline people the tools they need to come off competent and confident to the customer.

When it comes to service recovery, remember the axiom, "At that point where the customer is most insecure or incensed, you want your frontline people to be the most competent and confident." The more you're able to work out the details of that approach in advance, the more recovery success you're likely to achieve.

Five Ways to Make Recovery Routine

1. *Eliminate barriers.* The more paperwork and policy your frontline people have to fill out, duplicate, circulate, and take care of, the less time they'll have to really listen to the customer and the longer it will take them to go to work on the problem in a way the customer will find satisfying.

2. *Train their response.* At no time will the listening and empathy skills of your frontline people be tested more than when they have to deal with an irate, dissatisfied customer. Give them training that helps them develop skills beyond simply smiling. They need to know how to listen, problem solve, and handle the stress of dealing with upset customers.

3. *Support and encourage.* Be quick to praise and slow to

censure. As Atlanta-based consultant Martin Broadwell says, "Frontline people need all the praise and encouragement you can give them. They get all the bullets anyone can take from the customers. Praise is the bulletproof vest. The supervisor has to be the one to give praise and give it generously."

4. *Separate praise and critique.* Nothing is more demoralizing to a frontline person than to have the boss say something like, "Pat, you did a nice job on that . . . but you should have remembered to . . ." The compliment is always lost in the critique, diluting the value of both and tearing away a piece of the frontliner's self-esteem.

5. *Always back your people in public.* When customers come to you with a complaint about a person on your staff, listen openly and nonjudgmentally, thank them for bringing it to your attention—but avoid a black-or-white determination based on "right and wrong." Find out what needs to happen to make the customer whole. Take care of that. Then, separately, calmly, generally in private, meet with the frontline person involved. Treat mistakes as opportunities for problem solving and learning, not rebuke and punishment. Forgiveness fosters courage and builds faith that managerial support will be present in the face of the occasional error.

> When it comes to service recovery, there are three rules to keep in mind: (1) do it right the first time, (2) fix it properly if it ever fails, and (3) remember: there are no third chances.
>
> —Leonard Berry
> Marketing professor, Texas A&M University

18

If It Ain't Broke . . .
Fix It

Don't look back—something might be gaining on you.

—Satchel Paige
Legendary baseball pitcher

There is no such thing as a perfect service delivery system. You know it. Your employees know it. Your customers know it. Even if your delivery system is significantly better than your nearest competitor, you have no excuse for resting on your past glories. If the last twenty years—and the Japanese—have taught us anything, it is that an organization can't afford to be self-satisfied and complacent today. Not if it expects to be in business tomorrow.

That means change, innovation, and experimentation must be a way of life for managers. Continuous improvement has to become second nature thinking and acting. And that means carrying a *big* tool box with two useful kinds of tools inside: information *getting* tools and information *analyzing* tools. The *first* line of information is your measurement system (see Chapter 15). But you can supplement that with other techniques.

10 Ways to Get Information for Improving Your Delivery System

1. *Customer surveys.* Face-to-face, through the mail or over the telephone (or through a combination of any two or all

113

Figure 18-1. Customer survey measuring importance and performance.

	How Important is this to you					How good are we at this				
When I call ABC Widget, phones are always answered promptly.	VI	IM	N	UI	VUI	VG	G	N	NG	VP
	5	4	3	2	1	5	4	3	2	1

three), ask customers to rate you on overall satisfaction, on the success of the last transaction they had with you, and on specific aspects of your service delivery system. Then feed the results back into your system. Be sure to ask both importance and performance questions (see Figure 18-1).

2. *Focus groups.* Bringing current customers together to discuss the good, the bad, and the ugly of what you do puts flesh on the bones of survey data. Customers can problem-solve with you, rate and rank the relative importance of different aspects of your service (the Moments of Truth that define the shape and style of your services in customers' eyes), and explain how different elements of a transaction affect their perceptions of you.

Employee focus groups work as well as customer focus groups. Bring a group of employees together and ask such questions as "What are our customers saying to you?" and "What gets in your way?" and "What should we be doing differently?"

3. *Employee visit teams.* Send teams of frontline workers, supervisors, and support people out to look at the customers' "points of contact" (with you as well as your competitors) from the customers' point of view. Their assignment: Bring back ideas for improving transactional quality based on customer experiences. What are the pluses and minuses of your service delivery system versus alternative systems when seen in this light?

- Gillette sends the people who make shaving cream and hair spray into the stores where the products are sold to get this kind of firsthand, customer's-eye-view.

- GTE Northwest, the phone company serving a large portion of eastern Washington and western Idaho, lets individual employees volunteer to become "customer advocates" for specific customers. They visit customers and make the promise: "If you can't get your problem solved, call *me*." Volunteers can come from any place in the company. What they learn is invaluable for improving the service delivery system.

4. *Customer visit teams.* As a "180" on the tactic above, invite users, buyers, distributors, and other types of customers, alone or in small groups, to tour your operations, ask questions, audit operations, or become "consultants" to some part of the design, development, and delivery process.

- Northwestern Mutual Life chooses five customers each year to examine any aspect of its operations *they* choose—at the company's expense. The report of these truly independent auditors is incorporated into daily operations and published as part of the company's annual report.

5. *Customer advisory panels.* Retailers often use panels of customers to help them anticipate fashion trends; electronics manufacturers look for feedback on design, standards, and pricing; utility companies study environmental and consumer options. If you're working for a long-term relationship with your customers, they should grow and change with you and vice versa.

6. *User groups.* In the early days of the computer revolution, owners of specific brands of hardware and software often formed groups to share information and ideas; in essence, becoming a living user's manual. Initially, manufacturers felt threatened by them. Then a few smart ones began to use these groups of dedicated users for information and design assistance. Fittingly, when Apple introduced its first Macintosh model, it did so to the members of the Boston Computer Club.

7. *Employee surveys.* Employees are sometimes reluctant to

offer opinions and advice one-on-one or in live forums. A service quality survey is similar to an employee attitude survey, but focused on (1) employee perception of how well the organization is doing in delivering quality service, (2) how current management practices affect their efforts to serve customers, and (3) what the biggest barriers to serving their customers are.

8. *Mystery shopping services.* Some companies specialize in playing the role of customer and giving feedback on your customer contact performance. The best ones work with you to develop checklists or evaluation scales based on your service strategy statement; some will even put their people through your service training so they know exactly how your people are supposed to be doing things. As a twist, you can use your own employees as shoppers as well. It is also possible to do comparison shopping of your competition using your own criteria for good service.

9. *Toll-free hotlines.* A good service recovery system almost always has a hotline of some sort. So does a customer-focused new product development function or a quality team with a customer-centered agenda. Customers who call in to register a complaint, make a suggestion, ask a question, or have a problem solved offer extremely valuable input on your service delivery system.

The key to making a hotline work is data capture and analysis. It is more difficult than it sounds to get people in Department A to work with people in Department B on service systems improvement. This is especially true when one of the departments is seen as the "complaint handling specialists." Incentives are usually needed. And objectives. And attention to detail.

10. *Benchmarking.* Started as a way to compare operational efficiencies with companies that have similar problems or challenges but aren't in your business (so data can be shared without concern for competitive consequences), benchmarking has become more broadly defined today as a way of looking for breakthrough ideas by seeing how others are seeing their customers. The original purpose of benchmarking related di-

rectly to improving a service delivery system by comparing operational ideas and numbers with a world class company in another industry. That is still the best use possible, but don't overlook the teaching examples of anyone's comparative experiences.

7 Ways to Analyze Information

The "magnificent seven" that follow are sometimes referred to as the core quality improvement tools. Memorize their names if you want to be part of the in group at the next chamber of commerce or trade group meeting you attend. But don't stop at name-dropping. Use the brief explanations of these tactics as a springboard to developing your knowledge of these tools and their application to your business. It's worth the investment in a book or seminar or long conversation with a quality-literate colleague to put these tools to work for you.

1. *Flow charts.* They come in two forms for your purposes. The most common is a detailed, step-by-step schematic drawing of your service delivery process (see Figure 18-2). A useful service delivery system variation is called the Service Blueprint. It helps you look at your service delivery through the customer's eyes to find the pests that are bugging them.

2. *Cause-and-effect diagrams.* Also called "fishbone" diagrams, this method helps you identify possible causes of service delivery system problems and is especially suited to small group brainstorming sessions, where you sort ideas about possible problems and solutions into six basic cause categories, as illustrated in Figure 18-3.

3. *Pareto analysis/diagram.* A way of organizing data—usually data about problem frequency—from the highest to lowest occurring (see Figure 18-4). From this form of analysis comes the Pareto Principle, or 80-20 rule: 80 percent of the outcomes (problems, sales, and such) come from 20 percent of the causes (scenarios, accounts, and such). Use it to sort out which problems to attack first.

Figure 18-2.   Sample flow charts.

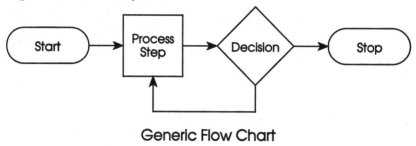

Generic Flow Chart

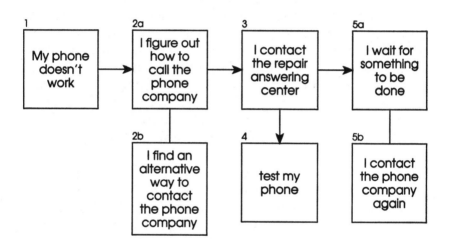

Section of a "Service Blueprint"

Figure 18-3.   Fishbone diagram.

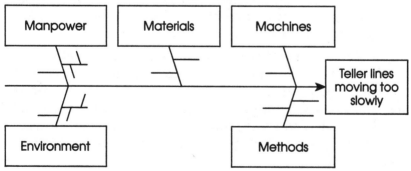

Figure 18-4.   Pareto analysis/diagram.

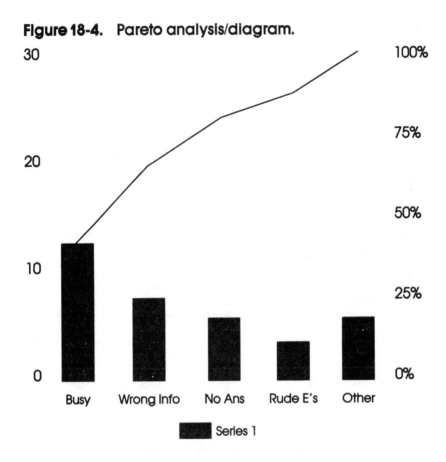

4. *Run charts.* Data collected over time and graphed for everyone to see (see Figure 18-5). On-time deliveries per day, customer complaints per week, orders filled per hour are all good "run chart" material. In classical quality control, a lot of time and effort goes into interpreting the pattern of the numbers on a run chart. A good one tells you if the changes you've made in a process are working.

5. *Control chart.* Basically a run chart with lines added to define "upper control limits" and "lower control limits" (see Figure 18-6). The space on the control chart between the limit lines is the range of acceptable quality. Managers with highly developed chart reading skills are able to anticipate quality

Figure 18-5.   Run chart.

Time or Sequence

Figure 18-6.   Control chart.

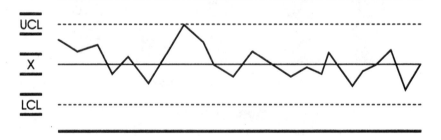

problems before they become an issue for customers by watching the ebb and flow between the limit lines.

6. *Scattergram.* A "plot" of data done to look for possible cause-and-effect relationships (see Figure 18-7). Say you want to know if there is a possible relationship between the hours an individual works and customer complaints (or orders taken, or dishes dropped, or any other countable circumstance). To check out your hunch, prepare a scattergram with hours worked as one axis on the graph, and complaints or orders or dropped dishes on the other.

7. *Histogram.* Another way of graphing data on the opera-

Figure 18-7.   Scattergram.

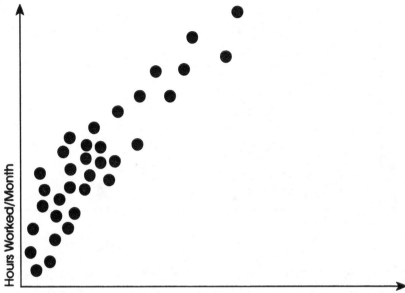

tion of your delivery system. The histogram is a form of tally sheet (see Figure 18-8). If you wanted to know whether there are more incoming calls in the early morning, late morning, early afternoon, or late afternoon, for example, you construct a running tally of incoming calls within those defined time periods.

With the continuing attention being paid to quality these days, you'll hear plenty of additional quality terms—tool names—thrown at you from time to time. If you're aligning your service improvement efforts with a corporate quality initiative, you may need to learn their meanings, but don't invest the effort if the new vocabulary will be little more than cocktail party conversation.

Do you need to know how to use every graph and chart and calculation and analysis technique to run a business with great service quality? Nope! But some of the tools may make it

Figure 18-8.   Histogram.

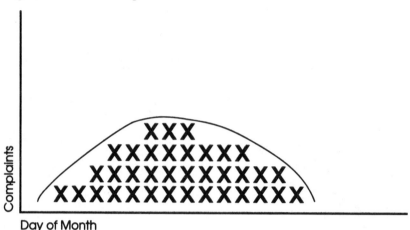

easier to improve your service delivery system and keep it clicking along to your and your customers' satisfaction. You *do not* have to be a quality control expert to deliver Knock Your Socks Off Service. But some of these tools can help you make the road smoother.

> Quality really is just doing what you said you were going to do. That's the most important part of the quality revolution, I think. Management has learned that they actually can do something about it by defining the requirements— finding out what the customer wants, describing that, and then meeting that exactly.
>
> —Philip Crosby
> Quality guru

Imperative 5
Train and Support

Learning is a way of life in Knock Your Socks Off Service companies. In the past, new employee training often consisted of nothing more than "watch John for a few hours, then I'll turn you loose on the customers." If employees made some little mistakes during their first few weeks, well, customers understood about breaking in new help.

That was then and this is now.

Today, a walk-in-off-the-street, start-tomorrow-at-full-speed match is unlikely. Your methods, policies, and procedures are unique. So is the way you want customers treated. As for asking your customers to tolerate on-the-job training—forget that!

...and when OUTFLANKED The customer rep JUST does a square-out into The secondary.

Knock Your Socks Off Service companies routinely spend the equivalent of 3 percent to 5 percent of salaries training employees—experienced as well as new. Managers believe that keeping everyone on top of changes in technology, competition, and customer demands is critical to success and survival.

Management support is equally critical to success in Knock Your Socks Off Service companies. Employees need to know and be able to see clear evidence that you are behind them in their efforts. They need to feel sure that you are on their side, that even if they make a mistake trying to do a good job for a customer, you will applaud the effort, if not the outcome.

Employees need to see themselves as colleagues if not customers in your eyes. Your personal credo should be: "If you're not serving the customer, you'd better be serving someone who is."

> If you train your people well enough, you can just get out of the way and let them do the job.
>
> —James Barksdale
> President, McCaw Communications

19

Start on Day One (When Their Hearts and Minds Are Malleable)

Coming together is a beginning. Keeping together is progress. Working together is success.

—Henry Ford

In the olden days of training, we used to talk about "getting them before they have teeth"—bringing on new people whose ideas and attitudes were open and unencumbered by a lot of bad habits and experiences.

- At that early stage of their job tenure, they were much more likely to accept our rationale for doing things in a certain way.
- If, however, we waited months, even years, before we started to try to build their Knock Your Socks Off Service skills, we often had the same kind of challenge orthodontists face when patients wait until they are adults before trying to do something about a gap-toothed grin.

Today we are committed to the importance of starting employees off with more than just the right technical skills.

125

Marcia J. Hyatt, director of employee development for Minne-gasco, a Minneapolis-based natural gas distribution firm that belongs to the Diversified Energies family of companies, says it well. "If we believe employees treat customers the way they themselves are treated," she observes, "then isn't it critical that we are as careful about the first impression we make on new employees as we expect them to be of the first impression they make on customers?"

If you believe, as we do, that actions often speak louder than words, then it is critical that we think about the entire new employee orientation *process* as carefully as we think about the basic program's content. Just as with our customers, we have to manage our people's initial experiences with the orga-nization. And its customers. Those first Moments of Truth on the new job can set the tone for years to come; they can, in fact, determine whether the new employee will be on the job for years to come or will have packed and departed in short order and been replaced by another in an unending succession of slot-fillers and seat-warmers.

What message, asks Hyatt, do we send to the new employ-ees who report for the first day of a new job, only to find their supervisor and most of their new peer group absent, out of town, in meetings, or otherwise occupied? What values are we communicating when we drop them off at their new desks with a crisp new employee manual, a box of no. 2 pencils, and a short course in using the telephone and computer system?

Hyatt's questions are more than rhetorical. The implica-tions that Marcia Hyatt raises are validated by some impressive research.

- A study by Corning Glass, for example, shows that a well-structured, supervisor-led new employee orienta-tion process can lead to a double-digit reduction in new employee turnover. That reduces hiring and new-em-ployee training costs, boosts retention of experienced people who have a broader and deeper idea of what the customer wants from them, and stabilizes work teams.
- A study at a computer company demonstrated that the time for new people to reach full productivity shrank

from five months to three for employees who had been carefully oriented to the company in general and their job and department in particular.

Traditions

Perhaps the best-known example of turning the new employee orientation program into a sophisticated process with far-reaching consequences is the two-day Traditions course at Disneyland and Walt Disney World. Every new employee who goes to work "at the park" is a graduate, whether they're going to be wearing badges that say *Guest Relations* or simply operating a broom and a dustbin.

Traditions is visible evidence of the extraordinary care that Disney takes to make sure that new employees understand the culture, values, and expectations of the organization. In the Disney vernacular, the world consists of only two classes of people: the "guests" who visit the park and the "cast members" who work there. In the Disney approach, new hires get a rare dose of reality as part of the new-employee orientation process. They're shown, in detail, how hot, tired, cranky guests are capable of behaving—and misbehaving—and given an introduction to the ways the organization expects them to handle that important part of their job.

An equally far-reaching, though less obvious, part of the orientation of new cast members is the way they are treated during the orientation program—and, indeed, the care with which the whole orientation process is structured. The Traditions program is carefully scripted and conducted in a comfortable, specially designed Traditions training room. Instructors are well aware that they are setting the tone for the way these new hosts and hostesses will treat guests when they make their first on-stage appearances. They're upbeat but realistic, supportive but challenging.

Does it work? Disney thinks so. So do its guests. So, too, do organizations such as Citicorp, Jordan Marsh, University Hospitals of Cleveland, Dayton Hudson Department Stores, and the Pittsburgh Pirates. These companies and hundreds more have sent their managers to Walt Disney World in Orlando to attend the Disney Approach to Quality Service seminar and learn how to incorporate Disney's orientation techniques into their own systems.

Good News

What makes a first-rate new employee orientation program tick? Two industrial psychologists, Kenneth N. Wexley of Michigan State University, and Gary P. Latham, a Seattle-based consultant, have looked closely at the growing body of research on orienting and socializing new employees. They draw three provocative conclusions.

1. There is indeed an important impact to be gained from doing it right. "Poor orientation programs," they say, "can be financially damaging to the organization because they can reduce effectiveness for the first few weeks on the job and they can contribute to dissatisfaction and turnover."

2. Orientation training should be the joint responsibility of training staff and the line supervisor. Specifically, they maintain that the training staff should take responsibility for communicating information of organizationwide, relevant-to-all-new-employees nature, whereas supervisors should concentrate on issues unique to the employee's workplace and job.

3. The expectations of new employees need to be specifically addressed. Wexley and Latham conclude that new employees, particularly those in first jobs, often have unrealistically high expectations about the amount of challenge and responsibility they will have on the job. Organizations, they suggest, must either make entry-level jobs more challenging or align new-hire expectations from the "get go."

There is a good argument that this kind of realistic expectation setting should begin even before orientation, in the selection process. It should continue through their initial experiences with the supervisor once they start doing the job.

Wexley and Latham have data to support the wisdom of making anxiety reduction one of the goals of an orientation program. They report that in an experiment at Texas Instruments, several groups of new employees went through a special, six-hour question-and-answer, give-and-take, getting-to-know the company session, in addition to a traditional corporate orientation program. The focus was placed on understanding the "real ropes" of the organization and what to expect from boss and peers on the job the next day. A year later, they found that these employees had learned their jobs faster and had higher production and lower absence and lateness rates than did employees who had gone through a traditional new-hire orientation.

Beginnings

Finally, there is the matter of what the new employee does when the "Hi! How are ya? Glad you're gonna be with us!" stuff is over and it's time to go to work. It is critical that there is real work ready and waiting for them. "Nothing is more frustrating to an individual full of enthusiasm for a new job than sitting around stacking paper clips," according to Wexley and Latham. Or, as Gordon Shea, author of *The New Employee*, puts it, "Don't put the new employee in the back room and tell 'em to read the policy manual. The new employee knows that's busy work, that the supervisor just wants to keep the employee off his back for a couple of days."

There is an old shibboleth: "Well begun is half done." When it comes to getting a new employee off on the right foot and tracking with your organization's service focus, well begun is a lot more than half done. It may well be the most important first impression you can make.

An employee is never more focused, malleable, and teachable than the first day on the job.

—Horst Schulze
CEO, Ritz-Carlton Hotels

20

Training Creates Competence, Confidence, and Longevity

Excellence is an art won by training and habituation. We are what we repeatedly do. Excellence, then, is not an act, but a habit.

—Aristotle

Nothing good happens for your customers or your organization until an employee makes it happen. Whether those employees are meeting face to face with customers or worrying over systems in the bowels of the organization, it is their skill and effort that make the difference between a Knock Your Socks Off Service organization and wishful thinking. Developing, honing, and keeping a competitive edge on your people's skills makes strategic sense.

It's not surprising, then, that in "service successful" organizations, training and development of employees are seen as a never-ending process that includes formal and on-the-job training, guided experience, effective coaching, targeted performance review, and strong support for learning from the organization.

Providing more and better training for your people can

and does create a big advantage in the marketplace. According to one study, employees who receive formal job training reach "standard" performance levels faster (72 percent faster), create less waste (70 percent less), and are better at customer trouble-shooting and problem solving (130 percent better) than employees who learn their jobs through the tried and true—and very inefficient—"sit by Sally and ask questions" approach. In addition, there is pretty good evidence that employees who receive a significant amount of training on a regular basis—between twenty and forty hours a year—stay with you longer and receive higher marks in knowledge, skill, and hustle from customers.

Training in What?

Despite its importance as a competitive advantage, however, don't confuse training with mother love, chicken soup, or high octane gasoline. It is not the case that if a little is good, a lot is better. Relevance counts as much as, maybe more than, minutes. To be effective, training should support serving customers better, working smarter, or creating better outcomes for the organization.

There are four kinds of skills your customer contact employees need to do their jobs well: technical skills, interpersonal skills, product and service knowledge, and customer knowledge. *All* are critical to their success. *All* need to be addressed throughout each individual's career with you. Following are some tips for developing and honing those four crucial skill areas.

Technical Skills

- Gadgets. Frontliners need to learn to work not only your computer system—software as well as hardware, plus associated devices such as modems, backup storage systems, and network linkages—but all of your office equipment. That includes the copier, fax, cash register (if you are a retailer), and the telephones. Yes, telephones. Some of today's systems would surely baffle Alexander Graham Bell—the days of POTS (Plain Old Telephone Service) are long past!

▲ *Implication:* Assume nothing about your people's knowledge of your systems. Even if they've worked with a similar technology, they haven't yet worked with your particular variation on the system theme. What they don't know can kill you with customers.

• *Paperwork.* They need to understand the purpose of your paper records and systems, not just which blanks to fill in with what letters and numbers, but what role customer histories, status, and incident reports, data integrity and privacy considerations, and forms filled out by or for the customer play in your system of information management. Any time that paper affects the speed, reliability, and personal attention provided to customers, your people definitely need to know your forms and procedures cold.

Interpersonal Skills

• *People skills.* Hopefully, you hired your service people for their abilities to listen, understand, communicate, and relate with customers as well as their technical and product skills. No matter how good their specific skills may be, the more practice, the more training, the more knowledge, and the more experience you can give your frontline people, the stronger their skills will become. The burden needn't fall on you alone. A wide variety of books, videotapes, audiotapes, and low-cost seminars exists to remediate poor skills and polish competent ones toward mastery.

▲ *Caution:* Training sometimes is met with resistance, especially when it is perceived as an attempt to "fix" problems people don't know or admit they have. Even experienced employees need their people skills brushed up from time to time—such training should be seen as natural and supportive, not a reaction to a deficiency.

- *Self-assessments.* Give your people a mirror in which to view their current performance levels. Encourage employees who deal with customers over the phone to record several conversations and evaluate them alone, or with the help of others. Use videotaped role plays to let them see themselves as others see them. Pass along customer comments, the results of mystery shops, and your own analysis and observations in a direct, timely, and positive manner.
- *Teamwork.* With a little training in the proper way to give another person feedback (see Chapter 27), co-workers can help each other brush up on person-to-person skills. *Do not,* however, make this a requirement. People are generally apprehensive about receiving a job skills critique, especially when there is a possibility that the news will be less than thrilling. It is a tough spot to put a peer or pal in. The secret is to separate performance from person. Focusing on the former builds up skills. Concentrating on the latter tears down self-esteem.
- *Self-directed training.* Give experienced employees the time and space (a couple of hours a month and a conference room will do) to role play different customer situations with each other, share tips and tricks, and generally talk shop. Don't attend these meetings yourself. The goal is for your people to learn from and with each other. That can't happen in the presence of the boss, no matter how "unthreatening" you think you are.

Product and Service Knowledge

- *Technical aspects.* Customers expect your employees to know more about the products and services you sell than they themselves, as customers, do. That's not always the case, however, which is one of the prime reasons so many people prefer shopping by catalog or direct services to shopping in stores these days.

- *Competitive aspects.* Customers also expect your frontliners to know something about the products and services your competitors sell. The more knowledge and factual information (as opposed to sales hype and "fluff and nonsense") they can give your customers, the less need your customers will feel for comparison shopping.
- *Customer buypoints.* Do your employees know what questions customers ask most about your products and services? And how to answer them? Do they have a list or file of common complaints about your offerings and your competitors products? Training can help them think with and sometimes anticipate a customer need or expectation.

Customer Knowledge

- *Customer profiles.* Your customer contact people in particular can never know too much about their customers, whether that involves the personal tastes of a consumer or the products and services of a business-to-business client. Your frontliners should be helped to develop a "style" for asking questions about customers—and write down what they learn. Customers expect your people to "stay told."
- *Heavy hitters.* Encourage customer contact people to create files on each of their five best customers, with notes on what they've learned about them. What common elements do they notice that are missing from other customers? Would nurturing those traits build business as well as customer loyalty?

Where Training Comes From

Knowing your people should be trained and getting them trained are separate issues.

• If your organization has a training department that delivers the type of training your employees need, that's a big plus. But that doesn't mean you're free to give the responsibility to someone else and wash your hands of involvement. You are responsible for insuring that the right skills are taught and that they are applied correctly on the job. (For information on how you accomplish all that, stay tuned for the next chapter.)

• If you are in a small company, or one with no formal employee training department or system, you are de facto the training director, administrator, instructor, and facilitator, all rolled into one. You can, of course, pass some of the tasks to a senior or lead employee. But it's not a "short straw" situation—training is too important to be done poorly or by people who don't want the responsibility. You and/or your trainer designate will need to learn how to do effective job instruction training, called "train the trainer" training. Local universities, community or junior colleges, and vocational/technical schools can provide you with such training or refer you to an institution that does.

Four additional resources are:

From the bookshelf. One of the classics is: *Training For Trainers: Increasing the Effectiveness of On-the-Job Training Instructors*, by Herman Brinbrauer, Institute for Business & Industry, Inc., Bensalem, PA 19020.

From the community. Budget to send one or two employees out to university, professional, and community education programs every year—with the condition that those who go must come back and teach those who did not. Rotate the role.

From your customers. Ask suppliers what seminars they run for their customers. You'll be surprised how many companies are using knowledge to build stronger vendor relationships. Get them to invite your people to come as well.

From your company. Ask people inside your company (from marketing and finance and accounts receivable to research and development and environmental engineering) to come explain their functions to your employees.

People in other departments love to tell their stories—and your people will be surprised by how much they don't know about the business of your business.

Successful Knock Your Socks Off Service companies are not only great performers, but learning companies as well. Their people are encouraged to be knowledge sponges, sopping up new information at every turn. They know you never know where you'll find an edge, so they look everywhere and all the time. You should, too.

The expense of training isn't what it costs to train employees. It's what it costs *not* to train them.

—Philip Wilber
President, Drug Emporium, Inc.

21

Making Training Stick

The five steps in teaching an employee new skills are preparation, explanation, showing, observation and supervision.

—Harold S. Hook
Chairman and CEO
American General Corp.

You fought for a training budget. Scraped together travel and expense money from the paperclip and staples fund. Sent your two finest off to a big deal three-day conference in Florida on the secrets of big-time customer service. Now they're back.

"So how'd it go?"

"Okay."

"So, what'd you learn?"

"Oh, you know, the regular stuff. But boy, that Disney World, what a neat place!"

"I'll bet it is. So, you took a lot of notes and have a lot of new ideas to share at the next staff meeting, right?"

"Well, ah, we didn't know, you know, that you expected a lot of notes and stuff."

"That's okay. I'll bet you have a lot of materials to share from the presentations. What were there, eight, ten different sessions?"

"Well, ah, you see, we didn't make a big point of grabbing up extras or anything. We were sort of, well, absorbing the experience, you know."

What they probably absorbed the most was good old Florida sunshine. And who can blame them? Whether you are sending your finest to Florida or your newest down the block to the corporate training center, if you don't prepare them for the experience—and help them integrate what they'll be learning into their back-on-the-job behavior—you aren't getting the most of your investment in employee training.

Send Them on a Mission, Not Just "Out on the Town"

You can't really blame an employee who goes off to a big deal conference in an exotic setting for confusing the opportunity to learn something new with a reward for doing a good job. Even a one-day seminar away from work can seem more like a holiday than a special assignment.

The "learn something new" agenda of such junkets will be much more likely to occur if you send your people off focused on what you want them to bring back and knowing why that is so important to you, and should be to them.

Here are three things you can do to make sure the people you send off to training get the most out of the experience.

1. Make training a highly visible event. Create a little hoopla. Whether the training will be attended by three or 100, make sure that everyone knows it is important to you and the organization. Hold a short meeting. Tell everyone who is going off to training and why. Explain what will happen when they return and how everyone will benefit.

2. Hold a pretraining "Heart-to-heart" expectations talk. Sit down with the employees who are going—one at a time—and discuss your expectations of the training and of their participation. Specifically, discuss: (1) what the training will cover, (2) why the individual employee is going, (3) why the training is important to the organization, (4) your assessment of the employee's strengths and weaknesses as they relate to the content and objectives of the training, and (5) how you will

help them apply the new skill or knowledge when they return from training.

If participants are going to be expected to share their observations with others on their return, that should be made clear and precise details discussed. "When you come back, I'd like you to do a ten-minute recap of the high points at the Thursday staff meeting" is a very different expectation from, "When you come back, I'd like you to present a two-day training program for the rest of us."

3. Assign pretraining homework. The last thing an employee scurrying to make plans for a two- or three-day absence from the job needs is homework. Just the same, preparatory readings, data gathering, worksheet preparation, and other training-related tasks can prime and focus the employee for the experience to come.

- Will the program be about dealing with unhappy customers? Ask the person going off to training to gather worst customer or biggest customer problems from coworkers.
- Is it a course on team problem solving? Have attendees interview you, other managers, or fellow employees about the greatest barriers to improving customer satisfaction with the team. (The people conducting the training can help you think through the best sort of homework to assign.)

Welcome Them Back—And Help Them Fit In

The training experience may have been great, the time spent highly productive and stimulating, the interlude just what the doctor ordered. But if nothing different is happening "back on the job," the momentum will die. Quickly. It's a more common outcome than you might suspect—the single biggest reason, in fact, why training doesn't "take."

The environment your people come back to must encourage and support their use of the new information and skills.

As a manager, you are perhaps the biggest part of that supportive environment. If you've prepared them for the program, you should have a pretty good idea what content was covered and how it can apply to the individual's job and the broader needs of your work group.

Often employees need help using what they have learned. This is especially true when only a small percentage of your people (or just one person) goes to training. Employees want to perform differently, but will need time, incentive, and practice to break old habits and make the new way of doing things second nature.

Back "Home'" Again

Here are five things you can do to help smooth the transition from classroom to real world performance.

1. **Debrief people when they return.** It may seem as if we are recommending a lot of chatting. We are. Letting people talk about the new ideas, approaches, and skills they have been exposed to helps the transfer to the workplace while reinforcing the value you put on the new insights they've gained.

The discussion should be more than a friendly chat, however. It should be fairly detailed and questions such as "How do you think we can use that here?" should play a big part. Let your people show you that they have indeed come back with something new and useful. Be lavish in your praise of the new learning and ideas, and the effort the employee has put forth.

2. **Hold a show-and-tell session for the department.** Asking people to explain the training content to others helps them solidify what they've learned. As every teacher can tell you, real learning takes place when you have to teach others.

▲ *Caution:* Some people would rather stand naked in a snowbank than address a group, especially of their peers. Find a different way for these people to share what they've learned (have them write up a two-page memo as an agenda item for an upcoming staff meeting or share a visual aid or handout from the session).

If you expect participants to actually train others—as opposed to simply delivering a general briefing—then special "train the trainer" preparation might be necessary. Good training always looks simple and easy—and it is, for the participants. But it's much more difficult to repeat secondhand, as a generalist, material heard firsthand from a specialist.

▲ *Caution:* You need to be ready to "protect" your impromptu trainers and their new ideas. Sometimes, other employees may try to "put them down" or upstage their presentation—a former peer who suddenly acquires highly visible and highly valued new skills and stature can seem threatening to those who "stayed home."

3. Hold a skill drill or practice session for the newly trained. We learn best by doing, but actual skill practice may be minimal in a training program because of the number of participants, the style of the presenter, or the inability to address specific concerns in a general session. If it is important to turn the new learning into strong habits of performance, then the sooner the effort starts, the better.

4. Catch somebody doing something new and thank 'em for trying. Making a new behavior an active part of an employee's skill vocabulary takes time and practice. It also takes feedback and encouragement. Particularly from you. Be sure you set goals for the use of the new skill: "I expect to hear you using those new closing techniques in all your phone selling efforts by the end of the month." Then follow through positively, with interest and encouragement, not officiously, with a stopwatch and a clipboard: "That sounded great, Lee. Keep trying those different closing techniques and I'm sure that by the end of the month you'll be booking all sorts of new business."

5. Hold a contest—a fun contest. Don't let learning to apply a new skill become a chore. Make at least some of the effort fun and challenging. Introduce some friendly competition or a lighter touch to keep everyone upbeat and enthusiastic. If, for instance, people have learned the same ten "closing techniques for telephone sales," you might have a one-day contest (perhaps announced, but on an unscheduled day of your choosing) during which you monitor calls and track the use of the new skills.

Keep it light! Make the awards small enough to be able to give out lots of them and invent a few off-the-wall categories to keep things fresh and unpredictable: an award for "Most Closing Statements Uttered in a Single Sales Call." Another for "Most Convincing Closing." Yet another for "Most Sales Actually Closed." And one acknowledging the "Strangest Closing Tried When the Customer Didn't Have a Clue What We Could Do for Them." Then, at the end of the day, reinforce the learning points by having everyone who won an award repeat what it was they had said—regardless of the category it was awarded for.

You can change behavior in an entire organization providing you treat training as a process rather than an event.

—Edward W. Jones
Training director,
General Cinema Beverages, Inc.

22

Thinking and Acting Like a Coach

I spend most of my time thinking about what will motivate players.

—Pat Riley
Head coach, New York Knicks

The definition of "boss" begins to take shape in most of us long before we get to the job market. It starts with "father" and "mother," then progresses to "teacher," "principal," and "coach." It may eventually include "professor," "scoutmaster," or "drill instructor." By the time we get to the work world, most of what we know about "bossing" has been shaped by people on whom we were dependent and times when someone else had close to complete control over our immediate actions and longer term destiny. Small wonder that "boss" for most employees is a four-letter word!

From Boss to Leader

Directing the performance of a service, rather than supervising the production of a product, calls for a different management orientation. "Leading" a service performance isn't directly leading in the sense of being that someone out front, with everybody else falling into line behind you. Rather, service management requires leadership skills more often associated with indirect management—coaching a team, teaching a skill, conducting an orchestra, directing a play. In high-performing service organizations, managers need essentially the same skills that coaches use to bring out the best in a performing artist or athlete.

Clipboards and Whistles

The similarities between service managers in business and coaches in athletics and the arts are many—and worth exploring as you try to give yourself a frame of reference for your managerial actions and responsibilities. Like a coach:

• *You instill fundamentals.* Your people have to know how to play their particular roles or positions: what to do, and when, and how, what to say, and why. Where to be when the customer feeds them a cue or throws them a curve. And just as great actors and athletes know the necessity of constant practice, of "getting in the reps" (repetitions) that help them master the part they are called on to play, you have to keep your people focused on the task and constantly honing their skills.

• *You build teamwork.* The second baseman is one of nine players on the baseball field. The violinist sitting first chair is just one player in the orchestra. No matter how individually talented he or she may be, the overall success of the production, be it the playing of a baseball game or a Beethoven symphony, is judged by how well everyone plays together. You position your players. You have to make sure they know how their role interlocks with others on the service team. You have to keep them focused on both their individual performance and the overall success of the group; keep the group working together in harmony in competitive conditions that challenge each in different ways.

• *You evaluate and adjust.* Every team, every individual performer, starts with a "game plan." But typically the plan can only prepare; it can't control play from start to finish. There are other variables, often outside anyone's control, that have to be taken into account in the midst of the performance. Like a coach, a service manager has to know how to reposition players, change the script, react to immediate needs, and anticipate circumstances that may be encountered in the next quarter or the next act.

• *You reinforce and motivate.* The coach's role is to plan and prepare, react and adjust, correct problems without destroying the player's self-confidence, and praise good efforts without giving the recipient of the "well dones" a swelled head. You can't play favorites and build a united team. You can't preach sacrifice and dedication and then go put your feet up while your people give everything they've got. Your words and actions set the tone for theirs.

• *You're on the sidelines.* When the manager walks onto the playing field in most sports, play promptly stops. It doesn't continue until the coach has returned to the dugout, or the bench, or the wings. Just as you can't direct the play from the balcony or run the game from the locker room, you have to position yourself as close as you can to the action so you can support your players without either getting in their way or being so far removed from them that you don't know what they need from you.

Preparing for Success

Before they take the field or the stage, players have to have a good idea of what they're going to be doing and how their individual performances will combine into a cohesive group effort.

• In sports, that preparation involves knowing specific actions to take in specific circumstances—with a player on first, the shortstop throws to second base on a ground ball to get the double play; when there's no one on, the play is at first base.
• In the arts, there's a script or sheet of music to learn,

often augmented by marks to hit when delivering a line or modifications to tempo and volume that provide subtle changes to the look and sound of the performance.

Business organizations prepare themselves in similar ways. At Disneyland and Walt Disney World, the young men and women who make the rides and attractions "go" work from carefully planned and memorized scripts, complete with exceptions, situational variations, and approved modifications—ad libs, in other words. They know where they're supposed to be, what they're supposed to do, including how to take charge of a potentially negative situation and turn it into a positive for their guests. Disney's service deliverers practice a performance art. And that theme runs through training and management at every level.

Matching Performance to Coaching Technique

Since the performance of your people is your paramount concern as a coach, your style and actions have to change to respond to specific needs.

• When your people perform well. The adage, "different strokes for different folks" is as true on the shop floor or the phone banks as it is on the playing fields. When performance is superior and the performers are appropriately challenged, good coaches search for outcomes (or rewards) valued by each individual and adjust their managerial style to the styles of their people. The key is to understand your best performers well enough to identify the specific rewards they value and the techniques that work best for them.

• When your people perform unevenly. Every coach is faced with performers whose play ranges from great in some aspects or at certain times to only average, sometimes less than average, in other areas. The appropriate technique is to reward the great stuff and to encourage improvement in the "only average"—but *not at the same time.*

When up-and-down performers hear, "Lou, you're doing great on *this*, but you can do better on *that*," they don't catch the kudos, just the "do better" part. Sometimes, in fact, they can interpret your compliments as a not-so-subtle bribe to get improvement—"I really want you to buckle down here, so I'll throw you a pointless compliment over there to disarm your resistance"—in which case, you risk losing the power of the reward as well as the focus on improvement. Separate the "reward" part from the "encourage" part, and you help your people glow *and* grow.

• When your people hit a slump. Not even the best performers can do their best all the time. Sometimes they hit a slump or a lull during which everything seems to go wrong. When that happens, remember the classic coach's axiom: "If I traded players every time they were off, I'd wind up without a team in a hurry."

Good coaches patiently communicate continuous faith in the performer, especially when the results have been off and pride, confidence, and self-esteem are at their shakiest. They focus on and reinforce "the fundamentals"—the good efforts that will eventually pay off: "That's the way to go, Ann. Keep that up and I'm sure your sales (or service ratings, or retention/renewal rates) will improve."

Much has been written about the power of the coach's expectations on performance. It seems clear that *demonstrated* belief in people translates into good reason to believe. If you think people will succeed—because you've put them in a position to do just that—and you treat them that way, you're not generally going to be disappointed. The reverse is equally true: Expect the worst and you'll have a very good chance of getting it.

• When your people try and fail (and *they* don't know why). This condition calls for the coach to function as a mentor. The Greek poet Homer tells us that Mentor was the trusted counselor of Odysseus (Ulysses), under whose disguise Athena became the guardian and teacher of Telemachus, his son and heir, while Odysseus sailed away to fight in the Trojan War. Mentor was known for his wisdom and sensitivity. Consequently, the word today is used to describe "a wise and trusted adviser." The challenge of the coach-as-mentor is to communicate wisdom and experience without creating defensiveness and resistance in the performer.

There are many aspects to mentoring. One key is to give advice in a manner that allows it to be heard, minimizes defensiveness, and keeps accountability for improvement with the performer. A useful approach to achieving such a tall order is to *first* get the performer's permission to give advice and *then* provide the advice as an "I" statement ("If I were you, I would . . ."). That's less telling and judgmental than an authoritarian "you should, you ought to, you had better" posture. Most performers, especially those confident in their skills and accustomed to succeeding, resent being told what to do.

Managers sometimes bristle at the suggestion that they should solicit permission from their people before giving advice to them. Who works for whom here, they ask. (If you're seeing your employees as customers of your managerial actions, not subjects on a feudal fief, the answer to that question should be obvious.)

The rationale is twofold:

1. The performer may actually know what to do despite your perception that he or she does not. Unneeded advice becomes unheeded advice.
2. This way, the coach keeps control and accountability with the performer, avoiding the surly look that says, "If you're so dang smart, why don't *you* do it."

• When your people try and fail (and *you* don't know why). This condition calls for astute analysis before action. A careful assessment of the performer and the performance often reveals unsuspected gaps in some ingredient required for high performance. The reasons for failure are many. Here are eight variables to consider in searching for gaps between the performance required and the performance being delivered.

1. *Role-person mismatch.* Reexamine whether the performer

would be more successful in a different role or on a different team.

2. *Task clarity*. Perhaps the performer is not clear on the performance you require. Would you bet your next year's salary that *your* view of their accountabilities and expectations matches *their* view of those key parameters?

3. *Task priority*. Sometimes failure is due to the performer's perception that the performance you expect is not really of high importance. Does their view of what's important match yours?

4. *Competence*. Failure can sometimes be due to a skill deficiency. People can't do well if they don't know how. Industrial psychologist Robert Mager offers an easy test to determine whether you're facing a skill problem or a motivation issue: "Could they do the job if their life depended on it? If no, you have a performance problem. If yes, you may have a performance gap no amount of training can correct."

5. *Commitment*. Failure can indeed reflect a will deficiency. Low desire or a lack of motivation can erode performance to the point that you get compliance, but little commitment. Have you given performers a sense of ownership and control over the work they do? Do they know "why" what you expect is expected (the rationale of the task)?

6. *Obstacles*. Real or imagined barriers can interfere with good performance. To the extent that you, as the coach, can modify or remove them, you can free your people to perform better. If you empower *them* to remove barriers, you build an even greater sense of ownership and responsibility among your frontliners.

7. *Reward for failure*. Sometimes there's more reward for poor performance than good performance. People who get attention (however negative) when they do poorly and are ignored when they do well may stop doing well just to get a reaction. (If you've seen a "worst performer" award become more cherished than the

"best performer" award, you've seen the dynamic in action.) You need to catch people doing well, too.

8. *Performance feedback.* Do you provide clear, rapid information that helps your people evaluate and fine-tune their performance? Is it useful and presented from a consistent perspective? Or pointlessly general and subject to weather-vane swings in emphasis that can confuse and disorient?

If analysis fails to produce a reasonable explanation for substandard performance and does not suggest a path to a solution, a sit-down counseling session—focusing on the performance in question, not the personality or psychology of the person involved—should be the next step.

• When your people don't try (or try to fail). The last condition of performance analysis is the most complex and carries a tone of "acting like a psychologist"—so tread lightly here.

This condition could be rooted in performer hostility— toward the coach, toward the team, toward the customer, or even inward, toward self.

It might be due to burnout: cumulative stress and the absence of emotional support.

Sometimes it occurs when people view the performance standards set for them as arbitrary or capricious, or believe that as soon as they settle in to one performance level, the standard will be raised again, systematically outpacing their capacity to keep measuring up.

If none of these scenarios is the case, and you have tried all the appropriate actions without success, only then should you resort to official reprimands to attempt to pull performance back up to acceptable levels.

Reprimands are designed to stop negative performance, but in such a way that performance can be improved *without* undermining self-esteem or leaving scar tissue. As Ken Blanchard, author of the *One Minute Manager* series of books, is fond of saying, reprimanded performers should respond by focusing on what they need to do to improve, not on how they were treated by the person delivering the bad news.

Most good books on discipline tell us that reprimands:

- Should be delivered in private.
- Should focus on performance rather than the person.
- Should be given with frankness, but not in anger.
- Should be appropriate to the infraction.

Good coaches do all of that and one more thing: They underscore the impact an individual's poor performance has on the team's performance. They know that it is far better to get people working to avoid letting down their teammates or letting themselves down than making them sweat to impress their coach.

The game of human achievement is played with complex players, changing rules, and ambiguous measurements. The coaches we admire on the sidelines at Saturday's game or behind the performance of a talented artist or performer have much to teach us that's relevant for Monday's corporate game.

> He is the smartest football coach who ever lived. He is very sensitive to other people's needs, and players respond well to that.
>
> —Bob Vogel on Don Shula,
> Head coach, Miami Dolphins

Imperative 6
Involve and Empower

Involvement is the enfolding of an employee in the decisions as well as the work of the organization. Think about it. If two heads are better than one, what could happen if *everyone* who works for you focused their brain power on your biggest problem?

Involved employees willingly think beyond the rudimentary features of their jobs and take on the role of problem finder and solver. But involvement is a two-way tunnel. Employees who are encouraged to be part of a problem finding or problem solving or new idea effort expect to have their ideas taken seriously. Any hint that an involvement effort is employee relations window dressing quickly kills commitment.

Empowerment is working *with* your people to enable them to perform beyond simple rules—to act intelligently, not out of habit, routine, or fear. Empowerment is neither a gift nor unlimited license. It is an act of development, a matter of helping employees feel an

Increased sense of control over their work, decisions, and environment in general.

"I'm sorry sir, I just follow orders" is the stock answer of an employee in a "don't think, just follow the rules" organization. "Let me see what I can do about that" is the signature of empowered employees working on behalf of *their* customers.

> Empowerment is the attitude that my actions are my own choices and the organization I am a part of is in many ways my own creation.
>
> —Peter Block,
> *The Empowered Manager*

23
Empowerment Is Not a Gift

Decisions must be made at the lowest possible level for management at the top to retain its effectiveness.

—Saxon Tate
Managing director,
Canada and Dominion Sugar

Bill had worked through lunch with the client so he could get back to his hotel to change clothes for an important dinner meeting in a nearby town. He was staying on one of those fancy upper floors, concierge level as they liked to call it. By 4:30 P.M., he'd made the quick change and realized he had almost half an hour before the client was to pick him up. Having skipped lunch and with dinner still several hours away, he realized he was starving! Not to worry, he figured. The concierge floor had a lounge area that provided small sandwiches and spicy meatballs to guests. A quick snack and a soda would tide him over.

Alas, Bill had not figured on the prickliness of the guardian of the concierge lounge. "Hors d'oeuvres," she informed him with all the pointless authority of the petty bureaucrat she apparently aspired to be, "are served from 5 P.M. We're not ready to open yet."

Over the rumblings of an empty stomach, Bill started to explain his plight. "It's wonderful that the hotel is willing to lay out such a nifty spread," he said. Yes, he certainly understood the rules, he acknowledged. "But since the chafing dishes are obviously already hot and full, and the plates and silver ready and waiting, we could surely jump the gun by a few minutes, right?"

"Sorry," came the reply in a tone of voice that made it clear she wasn't. "I have my rules. You'll just have to miss out, I guess." And with that, three very bright, positive days in that hotel turned ugly brown, done in by an employee more concerned with policies and procedures than serving and satisfying customers. Bill hasn't been back to that hotel since, nor will he be stopping by anytime soon. He's taking his business someplace else these days.

Was the woman genuinely nasty, mean, and awful? Or just another unempowered employee, afraid all heck would break loose if she passed out a single meatball twenty minutes before the posted time? It's hard to know from the here and now. But we do know that genuinely empowered frontline employees are the ones who most genuinely delight in shaving this corner and bending that minor rule to make a customer happy. And the managers of genuinely empowered people are the ones most prone to aid and abet them at every turn.

What Empowerment Is—and Is Not

There is a new fear shared by many managers in the 1990s: a fear of the "E" word—*empowerment*. They have heard one too many speaker and seen one too many film suggesting that "empowered employees" are simply inmates placed in charge of the asylum, set forth unbounded by rules to "do whatever it takes to make the customer happy."

What are they afraid of? The predictable things, of course: that employees who are turned loose will give the store away; that they'll try to buy customer satisfaction at the expense of profit, ducking the hard and nasty work of telling a customer no when that's the right (or only) answer while they hide behind the fiscally suicidal motto: "Whatever it takes to make the customer happy they can have."

Our experience (and we've yet to encounter anyone whose

EMPOWERMENT IS . . .

• Something you encourage	NOT	Something you give
• Congruence	NOT	Compliance
• Consistency	NOT	Conformance
• Accepted	NOT	Assigned
• Partnership	NOT	Parental
• Values oriented	NOT	Rules oriented
• Right things	NOT	Easy things
• Appropriately	NOT	Correctly

---

own experience doesn't agree) has been that customer service people seldom do such things—if they are well trained and managed, and if empowering them is a process, rather than a pronouncement.

Empowerment is the self-generated exercising of professional judgment and discretion on the customer's behalf. It is doing what needs to be done rather than simply doing what one has been told to routinely do. From the manager's perspective, empowerment is a key element in the process of releasing the expression of personal power at the front lines. It is the opposite of enslavement.

Because personal power is already present within the individual, empowerment is not a gift one gives to another. To the contrary, personal power is released when managers and supervisors remove the barriers that prevent its expression. The distinction is important because it focuses us more on what we take away from the system than what we give to our people.

What does empowerment look like? An empowered act, by definition, is exercising initiative beyond or outside the conventional norm. Confidently following the policy may be appropriate, and quite frequently satisfying, to a customer seeking nothing more than the standard offering. But it is not an empowered act.

Empowerment kicks in when the customer's long-term loyalty is at risk because of an unforeseen problem or unanticipated request. It's also at work in the little value-addeds that can make the most ordinary of service transactions extraordinarily memorable and positive for the customer.

E Is for Excellence

Empowerment, we're beginning to discover, has many benefits:

- An empowered employee can more effectively manage the customer relationship and turn superficial contact into a true partnership than one who must constantly balance professional instincts against the fine print of a policy and procedure manual.
- To the customer, an empowered employee is a powerful commentary on the whole service orientation of the organization. No one enjoys encounters of the "I'll have to ask my manager" kind. Empowered people say that the business truly is driven by customer satisfaction.
- To the employee, empowerment has significant effects on self-esteem and morale and carries a strong message about management's priorities and behavioral style. As University of Maryland's Benjamin Schneider has repeatedly demonstrated: Treat your people like gold—or dirt—and they'll treat the customer accordingly.

Today, more than ever before, we want and need people whose sense of responsibility to serve the customer takes precedence over a jumble of organizational rigamarole. It's up to managers to strip away the layers of organizational inertia that have calcified over the years so people can do that in a professional way that benefits themselves, their customers, and the organization.

Making It/Letting It Happen

"How do I empower my employees?" is a question as flawed as "How do I motivate my employees?" In fact, it is more flawed, since eliminating "boss control" is at the core of empowerment and the "how do I" part of the question, no matter how well intended, still reeks of "boss control." So where and how does real empowerment start? And what can a manager do to see that it starts at all? A short story will help explain the forces at work.

A patient at St. Luke's Medical Center in Milwaukee lost an inexpensive but favorite pair of slippers during his stay. Housekeeping, after learning of the man's complaint, concluded that someone had mistakenly thrown out the slippers and was quick to offer a heartfelt apology. Not good enough. Offers to pay for the patient's slippers also were not satisfactory. The patient wanted *those* slippers.

At that point, the traditional response would likely have been a diplomatically insipid form letter saying something along the lines of "Thank you for bringing this matter to our attention. Your satisfaction is our only goal. If we can ever . . ." and making it clear that reasonable people had done all that could reasonably be expected over a pair of slippers. End of story.

Instead, a young part-time housekeeper who had been involved in some of the phone calls over the incident took over. Acting on his own and not on a managerial directive, he got a detailed description of the slippers from the patient, left work, went to a store, and, using his own money, purchased a replacement pair of identical slippers.

The patient was surprised. And elated. And the young part-time housekeeper? He received St. Luke's first ever award for the most meritorious act of empowered behavior. It's called the Golden Slipper Award.

That's what empowerment looks like. No one "gave" permission for the housekeeper to leave work to go buy slippers. He exercised the personal power he had always had on the customer's behalf. He thought first and foremost about what was really at issue—a pair of slippers, not assessing internal blame or hewing to the strict interpretation of hospital policy over patient claims of lost items.

By choosing to celebrate his action on an organizational scale, managers at St. Luke's are now sending the message that this kind of behavior is not aberrant or suspect. It's an example of what everyone can and should do if St. Luke's is to continue to attract patients.

> Our people in the plants are responsible for their own output and its quality. We expect them to act like owners.
>
> —Ken Iverson
> CEO, Nucor Corporation

24

Removing the Barriers to Empowerment

No one makes you inferior without your permission.

—Eleanor Roosevelt

The customer walked into a crowded fast-food restaurant and ordered a sandwich, small fries, and soft drink to go. Told there would be a short wait, he stepped aside while the counter clerk waited on others. By the time half a dozen customer had worked their way past him, he was losing patience. Fast food, eh?

Finally, his slow burn now beginning to fog nearby windows, his takeout order was ready. As he stepped to the counter, prepared to provide a little direct feedback on his service experience, he was met with his bag, a confident smile, and a surprise: "I'm very sorry you had to wait," said the high school student who had taken his order. "I know you're in a hurry. Because you had to wait, I gave you a large order of fries. I hope you'll come back real soon."

Anger? Gone. Impression? Positive. What kind of place is this, where seventeen-year-olds can diagnose and disarm upset customers on the spot, on their own—and apparently with no need to protect the return on the restaurant's potato investment?

It's a Hardee's, actually. One of thousands where they teach people, "Don't fight, make it right." The extra fries didn't disappear into the inventory ozone. They were accounted for—

on a pad of "Saved Customer" forms. Built into the Hardee's approach to fast food is a recognition that customers have plenty of alternatives these days and a conscious decision that an extra helping of fries, a larger soft drink, or an occasional cookie on the house is a relatively inexpensive but very effective way to make sure they come back again when things don't quite turn out right.

Notice that the responsibility for turning that corporate mindset into action rests squarely on the shoulders of the seventeen-year-olds (and thirty-four-year-olds, and sixty-three-year-olds) who work the counters and the drive-throughs, typically at or near minimum wage pay scales and without benefit of a couple of years in an MBA program. How does Hardee's give that sense of empowerment to those kind of frontline workers?

It doesn't. The power is already there with the people who tally the orders and bag the food and fill the soft drink cups. What Hardee's has done is remove the barriers that prevent frontline service professionals from taking action when their own observations of what their customer is experiencing tell them that action is indicated.

If *your* employees come to work with adequate power to act with responsible freedom, what prevents this power from being used? Something obviously gets in the way. The key to the manager's role *vis à vis* empowerment is found in understanding the barriers and then working to remove them.

The task at hand is to encourage the directed use of responsible freedom on the customer's behalf. The challenge is one of coordination: getting employees to act with responsible freedom *and* in ways that benefit the customer plus the organization. It's not an impossible quest. Here are four consistent reasons that frontline employees fail to act in empowered ways—four "P" words that sum up the ways organizations have in the past effectively said no to their people's empowered instincts: no purpose, no protection, no permission, and no proficiency.

No Purpose

People will act with power if they experience a greater purpose in their work than simply the day-to-day task. For frontline employees to act with extraordinary zeal, they must believe that it is their purpose to "make a customer happy" or to "make the service or product work like it's supposed to." Purpose is the "Oh, so *that's* why I'm here" explanation that energizes and motivates.

Federal Express founder and chairman Fred Smith tells his employees, "We transport the most important cargo in the world—an organ for a vital transplant, a gift for a special ceremony, a factory part that may have halted a major enterprise." No story better illustrates how purpose permeates his organization than FedEx's role in the rescue of Jessica McClure, the little Texas girl trapped in a well several years ago. The Federal Express agent who received the late night request to arrange transport for the specialized heavy drilling equipment that was needed to sink a shaft beside the trapped girl immediately dispatched a standby FedEx jet. At that moment, that drill was the most precious cargo in the world and her first priority was to see it delivered ASAP, not to delay and hide behind the barrier of determining who would foot the bill. No one within Federal Express views that as out of the ordinary.

What you can do:

1. Talk about your vision often. Focus on what you want the organization to *be*, not just what you want it to *do*.
2. When communicating expectations, describe the "whys" as well as the "whats" and "whens."
3. Recognize corporate heroes by "telling their stories"— the details of their special accomplishments that become examples for others to follow.
4. Live the mission by making sure your daily actions are consistent with the purpose you've set for your people. Examine how you spend your time, what you show excitement about, what you worry about. Your actions telegraph your true priorities to those around you.

No Protection

Jerry Harvey, an iconoclastic professor at George Washington University, maintains that resistance to change is a myth. "It is not change people resist; it is the prediction of pain," says Harvey. A consistent barrier to employees acting with power is their prediction of pain: "If I slip or fall, no safety net will catch me."

As a manager, you need to reduce the risk factor your employees may associate with empowered actions. Even if it makes you tense up and cross your fingers to think of them out there on the high wire, your job is to reinforce their courage and commitment so they go out and try again.

What you can do:

1. Examine your procedures. Employees may feel unprotected due to past practice. Punish an infraction and, if you are not careful, you will create a precedent. Are employees clear on what is a "thou shalt not . . ." and what is an "it would be better if you didn't . . ."
2. Recall the last few times an employee made an honest mistake. Was the error met with rebuke and guilt, or was the mistake treated as an opportunity for problem-solving and growth? Is forgiveness for mistakes directly spoken or just tacitly implied?
3. Are employees publicly given the benefit of the doubt? If employees were interviewed by an outsider, would they say they received more coaching or more critiquing? How many times do employees get praised for gallant efforts that failed to pan out as planned?
4. Are employees commended for seeking assistance from others, including those in superior positions? Managers should be a helpful resource on call as needed, not a troll lurking under an organizational bridge and better left undisturbed.

No Permission

As a manager, you need to continually and explicitly give your people permission to act on the customer's behalf. It's dangerous to assume that employees will just know what they are and aren't allowed to do—or even that they'll believe you the first time you say, "Yes, you can." Employees have been hearing managers say no for generations through their experiences as customers as well as their on-the-job encounters. Empowerment takes some getting used to. As an executive at US West explained the change in doing business pre- and post-breakup: "Overnight, we went from a business in the business of saying no, a public utility, to a business that had to learn how to say yes."

What you can do:

1. Take to heart a line on the menu in McGuffey's restaurants: "The answer is yes, what's the question?" Apply that kind of thinking with your people.
2. Model responsible freedom and measured risk taking through your actions. Where you lead by example, others will follow.
3. Examine your reward and recognition practices. Which is more valued: creativity or compliance? Being adroit and resourceful or being accurate and right? Who gets praised or promoted—and for what?
4. Use "zero-based" rule budgeting. If you eliminated all the rules, regulations, and policies attached to your employees' roles, and then added back only those absolutely relevant, would you be writing restrictions long into the night?

No Proficiency

"Knowledge is power," said English poet Francis Bacon. The capacity to find clever, resourceful, and creative solutions is the mark of a wise person prepared and empowered to go beyond the traditional, the familiar, and the ordinary. Training your people, not once but constantly, provides not just competence but wisdom. And whereas competence promotes confidence, wisdom fosters power.

Author Malcolm Knowles tells the story of a medium-size manufacturer of radios and televisions that realized the electronics industry was on the eve of a sizable transition from vacuum tube to transistor technology. The company began to train heavily—even in courses that would not be approved according to most tuition refund policies. When the industry began to change over to transistors, this company quickly grabbed the dominant market share in the electronic appliance world. The company is Sony.

One reason that Sony's top brass gave for the company's meteoric rise was learning. They reasoned that the more people learned, the better learners they would become and the more likely they would want to learn. Sure enough, Sony employees learned new transistor skills at a much faster pace than their competitors. In addition, the more they learned, the more empowered employees felt. They had the courage needed to risk exploring new techniques and alternative approaches.

What you can do:

1. Emphasize proficiency, both by recognizing and rewarding those in your work group whose performance stands out and by using them as mentors and team leaders.
2. Be a lifelong learner yourself. Again, the example you set is the one your people will follow.
3. Develop a folklore of empowerment stories—anecdotal evidence that communicates (1) that empowered actions should be taken and (2) specific examples of how it may be done.

Our employees probably make more decisions in the hallways than most companies make behind closed doors.

—John Oren
President, Eastway Delivery Service

Imperative 7:
Recognize, Reward, and Celebrate Success

Creating Knock Your Socks Off Service is a human endeavor. It happens when a group of people willingly and enthusiastically work together to create something none could accomplish alone. Human nature is a key factor. Understand it and respect it and it will work for you. Disregard it, ignore it, downplay its impact, and it will work against you.

The people who work for and with you want to do a good job. They want to work for an organization and in a department that is successful. They need something back in return. They need to know how they are doing: whether they are succeeding or failing, are average or exemplary, and what they can do to improve when improvement is needed.

They need to be recognized and rewarded for both their accomplishments and their efforts—sometimes individually and sometimes as a part of a group effort.

And they need to be enfolded in something beyond their own ability to achieve through celebration of the effort and achievements of the corporate "all of us together."

A well-placed "well done" is the most powerful motivator a manager has—and the least used.

—Thomas Connellan
How To Grow People Into Self-Starters

25

Recognition and Reward: Fueling the Fires of Service Success

Recognition drives the human engine.

—Leonard Berry,
Texas A&M University

"Catch somebody doing something right today" is an admonition that succinctly captures years of managerial wisdom and a ton of behavioral science research. It has special meaning and import for the service management effort. If you want people in your organization to think and act in customer-oriented ways, seek out ways to catch them doing just that, and reward and recognize them for making the effort.

It is a reasonable and rational guideline, a precept hard to disagree with—and one more easily broken than kept. The biggest problem, of course, is that in the modern service workplace, most managers seldom see more than a small sample of employee behavior, and therefore have few opportunities to personally catch employees, particularly frontline employees, doing *anything*—good, bad, or indifferent. You have to be prepared to use what you see as well as find ways to see more.

Effective recognition and reward oil the wheels of willing cooperation and dedication to the job.

- *Reward* typically connotes money: salary and bonuses, cash awards, financial incentives, and other tangible payoffs in lieu of cash (though often chosen and presented in terms of their cash value).
- *Recognition* is typically less tangible, given for taking a little extra time with a customer, for going a step beyond nominal expectations, for caring about what the customer needs and expects to be done, and looking for ways to do it better, faster, smarter.

From Practice to Program

Recognition and reward come in as many styles as there are recognizers and rewarders. Common approaches include:

- High-profile formal. Programs such as "Lightning Strikes" (IBM), "Bravo Zulu" (Federal Express), "Count On Me" (Southern Bell), "Great Performers" (American Express), and "Thumbs Up!" (Citicorp Savings) come complete with detailed rules and objectives that everyone learns and set prizes, payoffs, and awards that everyone can strive for.

> ▲ Caution: Make sure your recognition spotlight doesn't put employees on the spot. If someone doesn't feel comfortable standing up to take a bow, respect their wishes.

- Low profile formal. Little rewards can be as effective as big ones if they are used in the right way. Lapel-style pins and special name tags are tactics common to service leaders such as First Federal/Osceola, LensCrafters, Citicorp, and Federal Express. At Citicorp Retail Service in Denver, good suggestions for new or better ways to serve customers warrant a "Bright Ideas" coffee mug or similar keepsake. The employee who submits the month's best idea wins a circulating trophy—a three-foot-high light bulb.

• Informal. A simple "thank you for your effort" note or a verbal "well done" delivered in front of co-workers are great ways of recognizing people. Style counts every bit as much as substance. A handwritten note from the CEO saying nothing more elaborate than "I really appreciate the extra effort you expended making the senior officers conference a success" is often more powerful—and certainly more lasting—than cash on the barrelhead. It's the sincerity and acknowledgment that count most to the recipient.

Seventeen Idea Starters

One of the best little reward and recognition job aids we've seen is an article penned by Harvard Professor Rosabeth Moss Kanter for the December 1986 issue of *Management Review*. Aided by colleagues at Goodmeasure, Inc., her consulting company, Kanter found, thought up, borrowed, tweaked, twisted, and collated forty-five different ways to recognize people for a JWD—Job Well Done. Here are the seventeen most interesting:

1. Create a "Best Accomplishments of the Year" booklet and include everyone's picture, name, and statement of their best achievement.
2. Name a space after an employee and put up a sign (the Sissy Jones Corridor) and an explanation of the reason for the award.
3. Show a personal interest in employees' development and career after a special achievement, asking them how you can help them take the next step.
4. Provide tickets to a sporting, musical, or cultural event (depending on employee preference).
5. Let employees attend meetings, committees, and such in your place when you're not available.
6. When discussing employee or group ideas with other

people, peers, or higher management, make sure that you give them credit. Make sure they know you make a habit of this practice.

7. When an issue arises in which a high-performing employee has shown previous interest, involve that person in the discussion, analysis, and development of recommendations.

8. Create group awards to recognize the outstanding teamwork of employees.

9. Write a "letter of praise" to employees to recognize their specific contributions and accomplishments; send a copy to your boss or higher managers and to the personnel department.

10. Send employees to special seminars, workshops, or meetings outside the company that cover topics they are especially interested in.

11. Ask your boss or the CEO to send a letter of acknowledgment or thanks to individuals or groups making significant contributions.

12. Introduce your peers and management to individuals and groups that have been making significant contributions, thereby acknowledging their work.

13. Create symbols of a team's work or effort (T-shirts or coffee cups with motto or logo, and the like).

14. Develop a "behind-the-scenes" award specifically for those whose actions are not usually in the limelight; make sure such awards *are* in the limelight.

15. Recognize (and thank) people who recognize others. Make it clear that making everyone a hero is an important principle in your department.

16. Take out an advertisement in an appropriate publication thanking your employees.

17. Provide a donation in the name of an employee to the charity of his or her choice.

Lasting Value

Sometimes recognition and reward programs take on dimensions that show you just how valued they can be to employees.

Several years ago, we worked with a theme park researching various ways to put feedback and recognition into the workaday life of employees—and improve customer satisfaction in the process. On the reward and recognize side, we started giving supervisors little cards called "Warm Fuzzies" to give to employees—you guessed it—caught "doing something good." Token givers were encouraged to write notes on the backs of the cards explaining what the receiver had done to merit a Warm Fuzzie. Four years later, we had supervisors giving out Warm Fuzzies, guests giving out Warm Fuzzies, and frontline employees giving Warm Fuzzies to each other as well as to supervisors and staff support people.

We encountered only one problem with the system. Hoarding. Not by the givers. By the recipients. Those "Warm Fuzzie" cards had point values—accumulated points could be redeemed for gifts and merchandise. But employees were not turning in the "Fuzzies" for the prizes. An employee focus group told us why. The psychological value of receiving the little cards outweighed the value of the prizes to many of the employees. As one employee put it, "When I'm having a bad day, I take out my stack of Warm Fuzzies and reread the notes on the backs, the nice things people said about me, and I feel better. That's more important than any prize I could buy for turning the cards in."

The solution was easy—give the employees credit for the points and let them keep the cards. (Made a mess of our research, but it worked.) The lesson was a big one: It's terribly easy to lose sight of how powerful a sincere "You did a good job—thanks" can be.

> The point of these contest and recognition programs and service evaluations and checklists is that they make everyone feel that service is his or her individual responsibility. That not only leads to better service quality for the customer, it also means higher morale.
>
> —Lauren O'Connell
> Assistant vice president, Operations
> Citicorp

26

Feedback: Breakfast, Lunch, and Dinner of Champions

Hey! How'm I doin'?

—Ed Koch
Former mayor of New York City

We all need former Mayor Koch's question answered from time to time, especially about our workaday activities. No one likes to do a bad job of the job they are being paid to do. Employees know work quality is the key to continuing to receive that valuable performance acknowledgment. As a manager, they look to you for the information they need to (1) recognize and keep doing what they do well and (2) understand and improve what they do less well.

Information that genuinely answers those "how am I doing?" questions—that your people can use to either *confirm* (call attention to good work) or *correct* (call attention to work that needs improvement) their performance—is called feedback. It comes in many forms and from a variety of sources:

- Some feedback is easy to get and hardly requires any effort to understand—charts and graphs of group and individual performance are fixtures in many workplaces.
- Some feedback is tucked away in the heads of custom-

ers—or your head as a manager. No matter how inaccessible it may seem, if your people need it to keep their performance on track, you need to get it to them, preferably while it's fresh and before it has been homogenized.

Display Feedback

Somebody once said that if it wasn't for all the statistics, baseball would have died years ago. True or not of baseball, it says something important about human nature. We love performance data—the more tangible, visible, countable the better. How high did he jump? How far did it travel? How fast did she run? Questions like these hold endless fascination for us all.

In business, we track shipments per day, deliveries per hour, pieces per packager, customers per register, and phone calls per minute. We love to know how we did all that today compared to yesterday, this month compared to last, in our department compared to a group in another building, or the people on another shift, or from another organization.

Through charts and graphs—the kind a normal human can decipher at a glance, not those multidimensional computer jobs that require a mainframe to make sense of—data displays give employees valuable feedback on their performance and motivate them through the mechanisms of "confirm" and "correct."

Dr. Thomas J. Connellan is one of North America's leading authorities on the use of feedback, recognition, and reward systems in maintaining high levels of quality service. He believes the best display feedback systems follow six principles:

1. Feedback works best when given in relation to a specific service quality goal. Goal-directed behavior is very powerful behavior. Tell a new waiter or waitress that they waited on twenty customers tonight and the first question you'll hear is invariably, "Is that good?" Good feedback tells employees not only how they are doing, but how they are doing relative to

the goals and performance standards they are expected to meet.

2. Wherever possible, the feedback system should be managed by the people whose work created the service in the first place: frontline employees. How many times do we put a staff person in charge of gathering, sorting, lumping together, and circulating information on everything from delivery time, widget quality, and scrap, to customer satisfaction and employee retention? The net result is that by the time such staff-managed information gets back to where it can actually affect the service delivery system and process, it's almost always useless as either confirmation or correction.

Given the right tools and a little training, frontline employees should be quite capable of gathering information on their own performance, putting it on a chart or graph, matching it against predetermined norms, and deciding whether or not improvement is called for. And when they do it themselves, they're more likely to believe the data, will act on it faster, and become more responsive to customers' unique needs because now they know "how they add up."

3. Feedback should be immediate, collected, and reported as soon after the completion of the service rendered as possible. The sooner feedback is received by the people it concerns most, the people it's about, the easier it is for them to relate their specific job behaviors to the customer's service quality or satisfaction assessment. If you were a driving instructor, you wouldn't wait until tomorrow to tell Peggy she just turned the wrong way on a one-way street. You'd want her to know how she is doing in time to keep you both from becoming someone else's statistics.

4. Feedback should go to the person or team performing the job, not to the vice president in charge of boxes on surveys. Obvious? Maybe. But check your current feedback practices. How long will it take for information gathered today to reach the people at the front line? Rule of thumb: the older the data, the less useful for changing the way things get done in your service delivery system.

Let's suppose you just now decided to order two giant

pepperoni pizzas as a lunch treat for the folks in the telephone bullpen. How well received will your little gesture be if first the pizzas had to be signed for by a security guard two buildings away, then picked up by a mail clerk on regular office rounds, and then brought to your office for your signature before you could take them out to where you wanted them to go in the first place? How good will those pizzas taste by that time? And will you really want to be their bearer?

If Domino's and Pizza Hut can deliver direct, your feedback system can, too. Immediate, direct feedback helps your people meet their goals and targets, in the process minimizing the amount of "looking over their shoulder" corrective supervising you have to do. Remember: Autonomy and self-reliance are key components of an environment that nurtures empowered frontline workers.

5. After it has served its immediate purpose, relevant feedback should go to all levels of the organization. Everyone has a "need to know" when it comes to information about how the organization is performing. But just because it's "feedback" doesn't mean it's feedback in the proper form or context. Senior management likely has no need for the level of detail that frontline employees and managers need to have to fine-tune the delivery system.

Asking "who is this information relevant to?" instead of "who would probably want to have a look at this?" is a good tool for eliminating needless paper shuffling. And the lower the proportion of useless information people see, the more attention they'll pay to information of value.

6. Feedback should be graphically displayed. The adage that "one picture is worth a thousand words" is certainly relevant when it comes to feedback. A well-done graph can give employees both the big picture and snapshot-sharp specifics at the same time. It also provides a readily understandable comparative benchmark for the next batch of information.

Do your people really want to know? Believe it! We learned that lesson at the same theme park we mentioned earlier. According to the folks in the marketing department—who had been keeping all of the info to themselves—there were wild day-to-day variations in guest satisfaction. After much deliberation, it was decided that "something needed to be done."

But what? After discussing good and bad feedback methods with us, John, the human resources manager, had a fifty-foot-long by ten-foot-high wall next to the timeclock turned into a giant graph for displaying guest satisfaction scores as measured by a thirty-six-item survey. Instead of batch-processing data, new survey results were added every day.

The meaning of the moving line was not lost on employees. In fact, in short order they began to ask for more detailed survey results so they could see exactly *where* improvement was needed. After a few weeks, the "guest satisfaction index" began rising. And though it took occasional dips, the wild swings in customer satisfaction were never seen again.

Troubleshooting Your Display Feedback System

When a feedback system doesn't work, it's often because the information gathered is being used incorrectly. It has stopped being feedback and has become a chore, a threat, or something to be avoided. Dr. Karen Brethower, an industrial psychologist, uses the following six questions for troubleshooting a sick feedback system.

1. Is the feedback being used to embarrass, punish, or scold employees? In one company, a "Rude Hog" award for the service rep with the lowest customer satisfaction ratings became a badge of honor. "Way to go Harry! Don't let the SOBs push you around" was the spirit it inspired.
2. Is the feedback about something that has no payoff for the people receiving the information? If there is no personal or departmental relevance to the information being collected, stop collecting it. Or at least file it under "nonessential."
3. Is the information being provided too late for employees to act on it? Too many things change too quickly for

weeks-old or months-old information to have an effect on meaningful responses.

4. Is the feedback about something the people receiving it cannot change or effect? You can tell a five-foot-tall person he's short, but nothing positive will come of it.

5. Is the feedback about the wrong things? Salespeople can't help it if customers think the store is inconveniently located or isn't decorated in a warm and friendly way. Get that feedback to someone who can act on it.

6. Is the information difficult to collect and record? Collecting and recording data can be a positive experience for your frontline people—unless the procedures are hellaciously difficult. We know of one company where employees rebelled against a quality improvement plan because they found the procedures so time-consuming that they were working overtime just to do their "real" jobs.

Good feedback is like a compass needle. It won't get you where you're going, but it will keep you pointed in the right direction.

> I honestly believe that the best way to get the job done is to use all the brainpower that's out there, to tap the knowledge and enthusiasm of the people who are closer to the customer than we are and let them show us better ways to serve—to serve them and to help them serve the customer.
>
> —William Ferguson
> CEO, NYNEX

27

Interpersonal Feedback

Printed forms for performance appraisals and MBOs are used by incompetent bosses in badly managed companies. Real managers manage by frequent eyeball contact.

—Robert Townsend
Former CEO, Avis

"How am I doing?" questions often have answers that can't be meaningfully transferred to reports in a three-ring binder or graphs on the wall. Interpersonal feedback is the face-to-face, manager-to-employee variation that is indispensable to an employee's morale, improvement, and growth. As with "display" feedback, interpersonal feedback comes in a variety of forms:

- Some will be based on your *opinions* or point of view regarding their performance.
- Some will be based on *standards*—more formal measures and efforts that define quality performance.

Standards, in turn, come in different styles. They can be:

- Written policies or rules—"Speed limit: 55 mph."
- Unwritten but generally accepted norms—"No swimsuits worn to the office."
- Specifically negotiated between you and your employ-

ees—"For the next ninety days, we need complete data in this format on the fifteenth of each month."

Which is better: feedback based on opinions, or feedback based on standards? Either. Both. However, as you might imagine, feedback based on your opinion or point of view is much more likely to be challenged by your employees, especially if they do not agree with the feedback.

- When the patrol officer tells you that you were clocked on the radar doing 82.5 mph and you crossed a double yellow line when you passed that car, there are objective standards behind the feedback.
- But if you are stopped for "reckless driving," your judgment may be quite different than the officer's.

Ensuring That Feedback Is Heard

The goal of providing feedback is to have it "take"—that is, make sure it is heard, valued, and hopefully used by the employee to continue or improve performance.

As a supervisor, you want *all* of your comments to matter. You know how to generate the information. But how do you improve your chances of having your people accept and act on it?

If you give feedback in a stern, parental way, you may encounter resistance because of the way your manner and tone remind your people, who now think of themselves as adults, of a very strict parent. By the same token, if you give feedback in an off-hand, flippant, "no big deal" way, your people will be inclined to view it as just that: "no big deal." The way you look and sound to your people affects how they hear, accept, and act on your message.

Two approaches can help:

1. Work from personal expertise. If your people respect your skill and knowledge in the area on which you are giving feedback, they're more likely to give it serious consideration,

even if they disagree or feel defensive. Joe Wannabee's over-the-fence feedback on how to improve your driveway jumpshot—which you think is a game-winner—you'll probably laugh off and ignore. But if your neighbor happens to be Michael Jordan, you'll probably give "Air's" feedback some serious thought.

2. Work from performance standards. You can't compel your employees to respect your expertise. In those cases, you can increase their receptivity to corrective feedback by basing it on standards whenever possible. This takes planning. You can't announce a new standard or expectation and then immediately critique performance against it. Employees need a clear understanding of your expectations and standards. They also need time to work up to those levels. Make sure standards are set early and clearly understood if you're going to rely on them for corrective action.

Giving Clear Feedback

Here are six steps to help you plan clear feedback:

1. Specify what the task is and why it is important to the unit or team. Discuss both the benefit to the team or unit if the task is accomplished well and the consequences to the unit or team if it is not.
2. Determine what other work is currently being done and mutually agree on how improvement efforts in this area rank in priority to other tasks or responsibilities.
3. Agree on a standard. Make sure it covers all elements of the task, such as completion time, quality expected, quantity expected, and decide which element is most important.
4. Discuss the resources (time and materials) needed for the task and agree on what actions should be taken to meet these requirements.
5. Discuss: (1) what you believe a person would need to know and be able to do in order to do the task well, (2)

your view of the individual employee's abilities, and (3) the employee's self-assessment of task and abilities. This is important. You may learn that a new skill must be mastered to achieve the performance standard.

6. With the employee, jointly establish the methods to be used to monitor progress, solve problems related to the task, and evaluate the final result.

Feedback is the breakfast, lunch, and dinner of champions because it feeds growth and success. Winners like to hear plenty of "you're the greatest" confirming feedback. Winners also know that getting better comes with feedback that helps them see their performance in the context of long-term goals.

Good feedback takes effective planning. It becomes more effective and powerful the more it is sincerely given and is based on clear expectations and standards. And like breakfast, lunch, and dinner, you need to provide it on a regular basis.

The wise leader does not try to protect people from themselves. The light of awareness shines equally on what is pleasant and on what is not pleasant.

—John Heider
The Tao of Leadership

28

Celebrate Success

I have yet to find the man, however exalted his station,
who did not do better work and put forth greater effort
under a spirit of approval than under a spirit of criticism.

—Charles Schwab

Celebration serves a variety of functions in an organization. On the simplest level, it is a form of recognition and reward. That, in and of itself, is an important function, a worthy purpose.

But celebration is also a way of nourishing group spirit. It represents a moment in time when a glimpse of a transformed organization—a product of the efforts of people from many levels—can be seen, felt, and enjoyed. In highly human terms, celebration reaffirms to people that they are an important part of something that really matters.

For most people, the feeling of being part of something important and meaningful is a powerful motivator. Being part of a "winning team," being seen as the best in the industry, achieving something others admire and respect become a power that can make salary increases, bonuses, employee-of-the-month plaques and even the most carefully designed perk program seem lackluster by comparison.

Celebration reminds everyone that purposes and goals not only exist, but are exciting, important, and attainable. Reconfirming to people at all levels in your organization that they are part of something important, that the service they provide is vital to both the organization and the people they serve may be the most important motivational principle of all.

Celebration should be an integral part of the way you recognize and reward good performance. To make it effective, pay attention to *when* you celebrate, *why* you celebrate, with *whom* you celebrate, and *how* you celebrate.

When

Timing is a key variable in a multitude of service activities, and celebration is no exception. As with other forms of reinforcement, "the quicker the better" is one good rule of thumb. It's hard for people to get realistically happy in December over something they did last June. Following are some good times to celebrate.

1. *When you need to mark the end of a project or major effort.* Achievers (those who take pride in a job well done) often have a need for closure, the knowledge that their efforts have led to a visible conclusion. When the work just goes on and on, lack of closure can burn them out. Achievers need to know they've achieved, in other words. In the absence of natural closure, invent it: "Fifty days without . . . ," "three quarters in a row during which we . . . ," the tenth (one-hundredth?) positive customer letter.

2. *When you are making a transition from one stage to another.* Celebration can not only mark the end of one phase, it can acknowledge the beginning of a new one, reinforcing new goals and standards with the recognition that the last ones proved eminently doable.

3. *When your unit has met an important goal.* Whether short term or long term, goals achieved in business should be like goals scored in a soccer or hockey game: an occasion for a few immediate "high fives" before the game resumes in earnest. Spontaneity is as important in celebrating as planning. Sometimes you'll have the champagne on ice. Other times, you'll just want to savor the unexpected moment in whatever way seems best at the time.

Why

Picking your spots is important. So, too, is having a reason for the celebration. Without a strategic component, celebrations can become trivialized or wind up reinforcing the wrong things. Following are some good reasons to celebrate.

1. *To motivate.* Celebrating obviously lends passion to the rational, emotion to the logical, and joy to the somber. It rekindles the spirit and leaves a warm glow that can endure long after the moment has passed. It pumps air back into the organizational balloon.

2. *To model.* Celebrations create a forum or setting that can be used to tell the stories of new service heroes. By making good examples of your people, others on the service team gain a deeper understanding of the attitudes and actions you want them to emulate.

3. *To communicate priorities.* Just as what gets rewarded gets repeated, what you decide to celebrate showcases your priorities. If the reasons you select involve cost-cutting, budget-reducing, and general frugality, your people will know to pinch pennies. If service excellence is the consistent theme, in contrast, you'll make it very clear that working for customers is at the top of your list.

4. *To encourage.* Sales organizations know the value of motivational sales rallies that renew the spirit of people whose job entails hearing no in every variation known to man (and woman). Service people endure similar stresses, and often without the counterbalance of sales successes.

Who

Celebrations are for people, by people. The human element has a lot of dimensions, including those that follow.

1. *Your role as manager.* This is one occasion where it's better to lead than delegate. Sure, it's important to get others involved. But you miss an important and necessary opportu-

nity and can actually send the wrong message by taking an "I'll just stay here in the background" position. You do not have to be a charismatic, back-slapping cheerleader type to lead the effort. Be yourself, but be up front—that's how your people know the celebration is truly meaningful to you.

2. *Their role as participants.* Basically, the more the better. There are times for small, intimate gatherings of a chosen few. But times of celebration aren't among them. Err on the side of too many people rather than too few. Let everyone bask in the warmth of success.

3. *The prominence of contributors.* Involve everyone who contributed in the cause for celebration. The key word is "contributed." You don't want to muddy the celebratory waters by giving credit to people where none is due, but you also don't want to recognize only a few of the many who played a part. It's even worth the risk of an Academy Awards marathon. For recipients, the chance to be acknowledged, and to use their "moment in the sun" to acknowledge those who contributed to their achievements, outweighs where the big and little hands are on the clock.

4. *The appearance of special guests.* You compliment your people and your guests when you reinforce the importance of the celebration by inviting others. Consider including a few key customers or vendors, or people from another department on which your people rely. A caveat: Defer to the feelings of the celebrants in bringing in outsiders—the unexpected appearance of someone they have good reason to label a "customer from hell" can throw cold water in their faces.

How

There's no one right way to celebrate. In fact, try to explore different forms of celebration to keep things from becoming routine and predictable. (You can, to be sure, have worse problems than getting yourself into a "celebrations rut" because of your continuing stream of successes.) A few guidelines follow.

1. *Keep it upbeat.* Celebrations should be fun, they should be positive in nature, and they should avoid things your celebrants find boring (such as the shopworn "chicken-a-la-Goodyear" meal and attendant boring speeches and bad jokes). Make the event festive and fun. Get lots of ideas by getting lots of people involved in the planning and execution.

2. *Use lasting symbols.* Find tangible ways to preserve the moment: hats and t-shirts, banners, a video that tells the story (or, better yet, lets those who did the deed tell the story), a writeup in internal publications, special plaques, or keepsakes.

3. *Make it classy.* Aim for celebrations that are public, not private; open, not closed; spontaneous, not scheduled to the minute; and inclusive, not elitist. They should reflect organizational values start to finish.

4. *Recognize and reward.* Pull the celebration together around the people and the achievements you're recognizing. Otherwise, it's just another party.

Some noteworthy celebrations:

• When Bill Daiger of Maryland National Bank wanted his frontline people to know that he and the bank appreciated their efforts to make MNB number one in customer service, he hired a hall, sent out formal invitations, and threw a magnificent party for all employees. The affair was such a hit that the bank now regularly takes time to throw a party and celebrate its "stars."

• At South Memorial Hospital in Oklahoma City, management found a unique and very memorable way to celebrate the hard work and dedication of the hospital staff. They created a musical comedy, in part a sendup of themselves and their behavior, and performed it for all three shifts of employees. Then they laid on and served up a special dinner—or breakfast or lunch, depending on the shift involved—as well.

• At Precision LensCrafters, they celebrate the end of store-level sales contest in a unique fashion. The awards meeting starts in a familiar way. Performance awards are passed out, customer compliment letters read aloud, and individual employees saluted by the regional manager. As the meeting winds to a close, however, a unique (and greatly anticipated) twist occurs. The individual with the best contest record closes the meeting by serving up a cream pie straight into the mug of a designated recipient—point blank, no ducking, no begging off—whopp!

Don't ask. Some organizational traditions and symbols aren't meant to be understood by outsiders.

> We have lots of celebrations. We create a lot of situations in which employees are brought before their peers and recognized.
>
> —Ed Crutchfield
> CEO, First Union Corporation

Imperative 8

Your Most Important Management Mission: Set the Tone and Lead the Way

It's sometimes hard to believe that you have any "power" over anyone in your organization. Or that very much of what you say, let alone what you do, has much influence over other people's behavior. But looks can be deceiving.

The people who think of you as "the boss" are more than a little swayed by your actions. Like it or not, you are the personal role model for many of the people who work for you. How they see you deal with and talk about, peers, colleagues, employees, and customers tells them what the real rules of conduct are for your part of the organization.

You can't con or manipulate people into doing quality work or caring about their customers. You *can* lead them there. Your personal example of doing things right, of taking the time to listen to customers and employees with patience, and focusing your energy on things that say "quality service" to your customers—internal and external—are critical parts of your leadership role. You, through your day-to-day example and leadership, set the tone and lead the way.

> If you are serious about product quality and customer service, and you're not spending 35 percent of your time on it (by gross calendar analysis), then you are not serious about it.
>
> —Tom Peters
> Management guru

29

Observation Is More Powerful Than Conversation

People learn more from observation than they do from conversation.

—Will Rogers

Though cowboy humorist Will Rogers had politicians on the mind at the time—and how their actions tell more about their real thoughts and values than any campaign speech or promise ever could—his quip has turned out to be true of most human beings. Actions *do* speak much louder than words.

There is even a body of scientific knowledge, which psychologists call Behavior Modeling, that speaks about the way the behavior of parents, teachers, super heroes, and rock stars influences the behavior of children—and the way the behavior of supervisors and managers influences the people who report to them, take instructions from them, and look to them for guidance, support, and recognition.

The message for managers is clear:

> What your people see you doing, day in and day out, sends a more powerful and convincing message about what is important to you and the organization than any memo you could ever write, any speech you

could ever make, or any clever saying you could ever
post on the bulletin board. The way you treat customers, vendors, your peers, and your employees sets
the "real rules" of the organization.

In short, whether you know it or not and whether you like it
or not: *You* are the message.

If your employees hear you talking about "those #&*@
customers! If they'd just take their darned questions some-
where else, maybe we'd get some work done around here!"
they walk away with two lessons learned. First, that customers
are pests. Second, that it's okay to treat them like the plague
rather than the purpose of the business.

If your employees see you chewing out another employee
in public, or witness you questioning a peer's sanity for trying
to accomplish something unusual for a customer, there are a
number of possible lessons learned vicariously. Things like:
"Don't put yourself out for a customer—it just leads to trouble
with the boss," and "Must be okay to hassle people when they
don't do exactly what you want—the boss does it all the time."

Hints for Making Yourself an Effective Model

Question: Want to know how to make your people better
             listeners?

Answer: Become a better listener yourself. Make sure
             they see you practicing active listening skills—
             with customers, with your peers, and with your
             people.

Question: Want your people to work better together? To be
             better team players? More cooperative? More
             prone to give and take and less prone to de-
             mands and "positions"?

Answer: Encourage and demonstrate teamwork. Become
             a better team player with your own peers. Re-
             ward and draw attention to good examples of
             teamwork when they occur. Treat your employ-
             ees as members of your team and envelop them
             in the practice of what you are preaching, just
             the way any good coach would.

Question: Want your people to deliver better service to customers?

Answer: You already know the answer, but for the book: be seen serving customers with the enthusiasm, skill, and attentiveness you expect your people to exhibit. And be seen treating your internal customers, your peers, the people who support your efforts, as well as the people who depend upon you for support—your employees—with respect, care, and attention.

First Union Bank, a subsidiary of First Union Corporation, Charlotte, North Carolina, was the most profitable bank in the United States in 1988. And one of the most consciously customer service oriented. But that hasn't always been the case. Not too many years ago, First Union had a pretty mediocre service reputation among its customers.

We asked Edward E. Crutchfield, Jr., CEO and chairman of First Union, how the bank went from just so-so to the status of an acknowledged service superior organization. He scarcely missed a beat at the question. His management "secret" is, he says, no secret at all. Will Rogers said it shorter, but he certainly didn't say it any better:

Service sinks in when managers talk and act service, service, service, day in and day out in obvious and in subtle ways.

30

Reinventing Your Service System

The greatest invention of the nineteenth century was the invention of inventions.

— Alfred North Whitehead
English mathematician and philosopher

One of the "luxuries" of being a manager is that from time to time you can stop, step back, and watch the thing you manage work all on its own. Without you. Without strings, mirrors, rubberbands, or first aid. It just works.

One of the responsibilities of being a manager is to use those rare occasions not only to admire, but to examine and challenge the same well-oiled service machine you so proudly manage. We think of that as a charge to continually find ways to "reinvent" your service delivery system.

In some Knock Your Socks Off Service organizations, that job is even formalized. At Disney they talk about "imagineering." Richard Johnson, manager of business and management seminars for Walt Disney World, is fond of explaining that at the Orlando, Florida, theme park, there is a vice president in charge of parking lots whose job it is to, among other things, find ways to "reinvent" the "parking lot experience" for Disney World guests.

Why? Because 70 percent of Walt Disney World guests arrive by automobile. Most of them with one to three subconsumers in the backseat, many of them on the end of a several-hundred-mile drive. All of them expecting to experience "Disney magic" from the first moment of contact to the last—both of which occur in the parking lot.

So the vice president of parking lots spends time worrying about how the lot lines move; worrying about how many guests will leave their keys in their cars, their lights on, and their motors running; worrying about how many times the tram driver should repeat the name of the parking lot area where a group of guests was picked up—so they remember later where to get off the train to find their cars.

The constant questioning—asking "How can we improve this experience?"—has lead to some marvelous ways of changing a common, everyday experience.

- Employees now cruise the parking lots in golf carts, looking for cars with lights on and engines running—and leave "don't worry, we have your keys" notes for guests.
- Tram drivers repeat the pickup point three times—to give us all a better chance of remembering.
- And there is a full-service repair shop tucked into one corner of one lot so that if anyone needs help in starting the family Hupmobile or changing a tire, Disney can surprise them with a little no-charge assistance.

The Four-Question Inventing Process

How can you reinvent the part of the delivery system you manage? It takes a lot of creativity and a strong belief that what you manage and how customers experience it are critically important to your overall business success.

To help you, we offer the following four-question "process" as a beginning. As you work through each question, keep in mind both your customers' needs (the outcome they seek—the product) and their expectations (how they want their needs met—the performance).

1. What is the memory you want your customer to take

away as a result of doing business with you? Stated differently, what do you want your customers' "love stories" ("gosh, I just love the way they . . .") to feature? What emotions and feelings are likely to invite the customer back?

For example, suppose you're the owner or manager of a small hospital. Since your customers (patients and their families) come to the hospital mostly when they are sick, hurt, or scared, you want them to remember feeling "personally cared for and about" after they leave—as though they were the only patient the hospital had to care for.

---

2. What other service provider has produced those emotions and feelings for you? Think of any vendor, store, or organization that, through the way it served you, left you with the kind of memory you selected in the question above.

The Radisson Plaza Hotel's Plaza Club in Alexandria, Virginia, is one place that has made Chip Bell feel very special and "personally cared for and about." On a recent visit, they not only had the room preassigned and a personal handwritten note on the dresser, but also had his name on the laundry tags in the closet and the matches in the ashtrays. On check in, the bell stand attendant called ahead and someone put fresh ice in the ice bucket. They even put a bookmark at today's date in the *TV Guide*. A week later, they sent him a handwritten thank-you note. Impressed by a first stay, his second was even more memorable. It was obvious to him that they wanted him to feel welcomed back, like an old friend. It created a very strong sense of being cared for.

---

3. What specific part of your service delivery system needs to be improved, changed, or reinvented? Don't try to take on every aspect of service you provide to customers. When you're trying to improve the performance quality of your service, the

more specific you can be, the better. (Just as you'd concentrate on Act Two, Scene One to fix a play, or turning the double play to improve a baseball team.)

From personal experiences as an overnight patient in a hospital, the wait and hassle of admitting stands out. The forms were long. The staff was highly efficient, but no one seemed very glad we were there. The sterile hospital room was about as homey as an army induction center—there was a TV in the waiting room and pastel paint on the walls, but the setting was not particularly full of life. There were a lot of stations to visit, and they all seemed far from each other. Worst of all, virtually everything, from the hallways and the waiting rooms to the people in them, felt cold!

Sound like an experience crying out for reinvention? The key is to stand back and experience your system as an outsider would. Places for reinvention will cry out to you as well.

4. How would the designer of your "great service memory" model (question 2) redesign the part of your service delivery system on which you focused (question 3)? In other words, how would the Radisson's Plaza Club design hospital admitting to ensure that every patient remembered the feeling of getting "personalized care?"

We suspect that if we'd stayed at the hospital before, the Radisson-designed admitting process would:

- Simply verify the information already in computer memory instead of making us go through a long, laborious registration process.
- Perhaps issue a special card (as at the public library) that not only would give access to a special parking lot or special lounge, but might even generate the paperwork while we parked.
- Ask what we would like to be called during our stay, what magazines we wanted to read, what kind of music to pipe in on the radio.

- Introduce the key people who would be taking care of us, and would do so as if introducing them to a friend.
- Alert the lab that we were en route so the attendant would be able to greet us, and by the name we'd asked to be called.
- Remember we liked strawberry and not chocolate ice cream.
- And since our "vitals" are in their computer, send a birthday card as a follow-up after discharge.

A Fresh Look

The four questions in the previous section are tools to help stimulate your creative processes. To use a now popular word, they provide a way to help you "shift your service paradigm"— a new way to think about how service might be delivered to the customer.

Notice how many of the supposed improvements to the hospital admitting process outlined above involve people rather than process: personal greetings, individualized touches, care and caring that are only possible if the people in the system are making the system serve the customer, not vice versa. That's why your people are front and center in this analysis— and in service in general.

In the midst of the fun and appeal of inventiveness is one important caveat: Whatever is created or invented must be grounded in what your customers will value and what your people can deliver. Before implementing a new way to deliver service, ask customers their reaction and involve your people in planning and piloting the changes.

That's how you "knock their socks off."

The mind of man is capable of anything. Because every-thing is in it. All of the past as well as all of the future.

—Joseph Conrad
English novelist

31

The Journey From Boss to Leader

Lead, follow, or get out of the way!

—Sign on a Marine Corps
Training Center door

Service quality is a journey, not a destination. Knock Your Socks Off Service is a competitive edge you recreate each and every day—each and every time you unlock the door and open for business; each and every time you or one of your employees answers a phone, fills an order, or greets a customer. Your only sustained advantage in today's marketplace is your last successful transaction with a customer. You win or you lose right there, real time and every time.

Management Isn't Enough

Creating and maintaining a Knock Your Socks Off Service edge takes great management, great marketing, great selling, great people, and great products and services. It takes one more thing—it takes you setting the tone and leading the way.

And there *is* a difference between leading and managing. Finding the right people, ensuring that they are well trained, have the tools they need to do the job, and that the system they work in is constructed for success with customers are parts of good management. So are watching the budget and expenses, measuring the performance of your people and systems, and being a player on the management "think team."

You can have a successful and fulfilling career being a good manager. However, leading is a different sort of life experience; a way of behaving as a manager or supervisor or executive that transcends managing.

- A leader is the sort of person—a special sort of manager—who is able to pick up the mood, tone, and tenor of his or her unit, buoy people's spirits, and enlist them in a cause.
- A leader has a vision of the future of the group—what it could achieve—and can communicate that vision to others and win them to the effort.
- A leader is willing to work long hours, without complaint, to realize that vision, and to serve as a positive role model for others.
- A leader is an energizer and, in many ways, an inspiration and inspirer.

Sounds like John Wayne with pom-poms, doesn't it? And you have great reservations about your ability to pull off a Bill Marriott/Mary Kay Ash/Lou Holtz "let's get out there and win this one for old ABC Widgets and the Gipper, who's lying there in his hospital bed at St. Mary's hoping and praying for you" sort of speech.

Not to worry. That's but one approach to—one style of—leadership. It isn't the only one. What is important and has to be at the core of your leadership efforts is this: You must believe in and enjoy what you are doing, have a vision you believe in and can hardly wait to see become reality, and be able to communicate that vision in a believable, understandable, and compelling way.

No one *wants* to work for a cheerleader boss—a visionless manipulator who simply enjoys the sound of his or her own voice and the thrill of talking others into doing his or her bidding. But who can resist the challenge of signing up to be part of a team with real goals, real aspirations, and real accomplishments before it?

Professor Rosabeth Moss Kantor of Harvard University has studied high- and low-performing teams. She believes that people are won to a common cause within organizations and work enthusiastically and collaboratively when:

1. They understand the *purpose* of their work.
2. They feel they are *members* of an important group.
3. They have a sense of *ownership* of their work.
4. They have high *self-esteem*.
5. They have management *support*.
6. They have *resources*—the time, tools, and training—to do the job they are being asked to do.
7. They have the *information* about what is going on, what they are doing, and how well they are doing it.

A lot of that *is* the product of good management. And some of it comes only from inspiring leadership. According to Dr. George Shapiro, of the University of Minnesota, who studied effective leaders around the world, leaders take five actions that put themselves and their followers on the road to success.

1. Leaders define reality. They cut through the confusion and tell their followers what to focus on. When you make a fetish out of counting dollars and dimes, you communicate "don't let customers get away with so much as an extra penny" as the reality of your unit.

When lawyer Erie Chapman took over as CEO of U.S. Healthcare and president of Riverside Methodist Hospital in Columbus, Ohio, he noticed that his new customers experienced much in common with his former customers in the American legal system. The hospital patient—stripped of personal clothing, removed from a familiar environment, and surrounded by drab-colored walls, institutional furniture, and unable to leave at will—experienced a reality not all that different from that of a prisoner in the American legal system. Chapman set out to change that reality by redefining the hospital reality to one in which the patient has power. At Riverside Methodist and the other medical centers in the U.S.

Health family, personal comfort, dignity, and preferences count.

2. Leaders endow a sense of mission. Effective leaders give their followers a reason to be part of the effort. If the best reason you can think of is "because you'll get a paycheck on Friday," don't expect enthusiastic followers.

Ben Cohen and Jerry Greenfield, of Ben and Jerry's Homemade Ice Cream fame, instill in their employees—and their customers—a sense of mission larger than a double scoop, extra fudge ice cream cone. From their commitment to employees' personal development and involvement to their commitment to "giving back" something to the local and global community, these leaders have endowed their company with a special sense of mission.

3. Leaders provide a vision of the mission. Through your eyes, the purpose becomes real. You don't have to be Walt Disney to provide vision for your employees—though thinking "How might Walt see this?" can help. Your job is to see the future—the ever-moving, ever-distant goal of service quality—and to make that future concrete in the hearts and minds of your people.

A sense of vision takes you and your people beyond the here and now to envision the possible future. Sometimes that's a hard leap, especially when employees get caught in the rut of "but we're already better than those other guys" or "but we do what customers expect and they seem pretty happy with it." Your vision will help your people "reinvent" what they do to and for customers.

4. Leaders offer a strategy of hope. The service quality journey is not always easy. In fact, it is often tough and discouraging. The new computer system you installed frustrates rather than helps. Your "best" customer tells you to take a hike after a less than model conversation with your most experienced employee. And you learn that your unit will face a significant budget reduction in the next biennium. This is the time when effective leaders draw hope and strength from their followers—and give it back fivefold.

In 1991, Cray Research lost a key supercomputer contract,

worth over $60 million, to rival NEC Corporation of Japan. Time to fire the sales department? Not so. Instead, CEO John Rollwagen sent a memo to employees reiterating his faith in Cray's product over its "technologically inferior competitors" and his belief that with a unified effort focused on meeting customer needs, "The competition cannot beat us."

5. Leaders set the tone/style/climate for their people. Your people, your followers, take their cue from you. You influence how they feel about the organization as a whole, about your unit in particular, about the type of work they do, and about themselves. What you value, they will value.

When Chris Cox, chief of staff for the New Jersey Division of Motor Vehicles, was charged by then-governor Thomas Kean with making the system work, she knew that she was faced with a complete cultural turnabout. Employees, used to being the butt of jokes and angry customer tirades, needed her confidence and commitment to see themselves as valuable and important rather than as secondary victims of an entrenched and unchangeable system.

Did it work? You bet. Visiting—and working—at the DMV is no longer the horror and trauma it was once seen to be. In fact, says Cox, "I've had to work on setting up a system to share complimentary letters with people. We've never had complimentary letters before."

An old Chinese proverb holds that the longest journey begins with a single step. When that first step is taken by an enthusiastic, focused, dedicated leader—all sorts of interesting things can happen along the road called Knock Your Socks Off Service.

> I find the great thing in this world is, not where we stand, but in what direction we are moving.
>
> —Oliver Wendell Holmes
> American jurist

For More Reading on Service

Albrecht, Karl, and Ron Zemke, *Service America! Doing Business in the New Economy*. Homewood, IL: Dow Jones-Irwin, 1985.

Anderson, Kristin, and Ron Zemke, *Delivering Knock Your Socks Off Service*. New York: AMACOM Books, 1991.

Bell, Chip R., "Customer Candor: A Tool for Partnerships," *Mobius* (Spring 1990).

———. "Nervous Service: Servicing Under Pressure," *AFSM International* (February 1992).

Bell, Chip R., and Kathy Ridge, "Service Recovery for Trainers," *Training and Development Journal* (1992).

Bell, Chip R., and Fran C. Sims, "Casting Customer Service People," *Supervisory Management* (June 1990).

Bell, Chip R., and Ron Zemke, "Do Service Procedures Tie Employee Hands?" *Personnel Journal* (September 1988).

———. "The Performing Art of Service Management," *Management Review* (July 1990).

———. "Service Breakdown: The Road to Recovery," *Management Review* (October 1987).

Berry, Leonard, David Bennett, and Carter Brown, *Service Quality: A Profit Strategy for Financial Institutions*. Homewood, IL: Dow Jones-Irwin, 1988.

Berry, Leonard, L., and A. Parasuraman, *Marketing Services: Competing Through Quality*. New York: The Free Press, 1991.

Carlzon, Jan, *Moments of Truth*. Cambridge, MA: Ballinger Publishing Co., 1987.

Levitt, Theodore, "After the Sale Is Over . . . ," *Harvard Business Review* (September–October, 1983).

Peters, Thomas J., and Nancy Austin, *A Passion for Excellence.* New York: Random House, 1985.

Schaaf, Dick, and Ron Zemke, *Taking Care of Business: 101 Ways To Keep Customers Coming Back.* Minneapolis: Lakewood Books, 1991.

Shostack, G. Lynn, "Designing Service That Delivers," *Harvard Business Review* (January–February, 1984).

Zemke, Ron, and Chip R. Bell, *Service Wisdom.* Minneapolis: Lakewood Books, 1990.

———. "Service Recovery: Doing It Right the Second Time," *Training* (June, 1990).

Zemke, Ron, and Dick Schaaf, *The Service Edge: 101 Companies That Profit From Customer Care.* New York: NAL, 1989.

About the Authors

Ron Zemke is a management consultant, journalist, and behavioral scientist who has become one of the best-known and most widely quoted authorities on the United States's continuing service revolution. As senior editor of *TRAINING Magazine* and editor of *The Service Edge* newsletter, he has covered the emergence and development of the global service economy.

Ron founded Performance Research Associates, his Minneapolis-based consulting group specializing in needs analysis, service quality audits, and service management programs in 1972 to conduct organizational effectiveness and productivity improvement studies for business and industry. His clients have included Wachovia Bank and Trust, Citibank, Marquette National Bank, Wells Fargo Bank, First Bank System, GTE-MTO, 3M Company, Ford Motor Co., General Motors–Canada, Air Canada, Western Airlines, Steelcase, General Mills, Deluxe Check Printers, the National Safety Council, Pitney-Bowes Corp., and Union Carbide.

Ron has authored or co-authored ten books, including *Delivering Knock Your Socks Off Service* (AMACOM), *The Service Edge: 101 Companies That Profit From Customer Care*, and *Service America! Doing Business in the New Economy*.

Chip Bell is a partner with PRA and headquartered in Charlotte, North Carolina. His consulting practice focuses on service management and training. He was formerly a partner with LEAD Associates, Inc., a training and consulting firm. Prior to that he was Vice President and Director of Management and Organizational Development for NCNB Corporation (now NationsBank). Dr. Bell holds graduate degrees in organizational psychology and human resource development from Vanderbilt University and George Washington University.

Chip is the author or co-author of nine books including *Service Wisdom, Influencing: Marketing the Ideas That Matter, Instructing for Results*, and *Clients and Consultants*, 2nd edition. His articles have appeared in numerous professional journals including *Management Review, Journal of Management Consulting, TRAINING Magazine, Personnel Journal, Training and Development Journal, Advanced Management Journal, Mobius, Supervisory Management, HR Magazine*, and *AFSM Professional Journal*.

He has served as consultant and/or trainer to such organizations as GTE, Coca-Cola, Shell Oil, Price Waterhouse, GE, Amdahl, IBM, BF Goodrich, Duke Power, MCI, Gillette, Nabisco, Marriott, Digital Equipment, First Union Corporation, and Precision LensCrafters.